Toward a Theology of the Body

Toward
a
Theology of the Body

Mary Timothy Prokes, FSE

William B. Eerdmans Publishing Company
Grand Rapids, Michigan

Copyright © T&T Clark Ltd, 1996

Published in Great Britain by T&T Clark Ltd,
59 George Street, Edinburgh EH2 2LQ, Scotland

This edition published under license from T&T Clark Ltd by
Wm. B. Eerdmans Publishing Co.,
255 Jefferson Ave. S.E.,
Grand Rapids,
Michigan 49503

First published 1996

ISBN 0-8028-4339-5

Typeset by Fakenham Photosetting Ltd, Fakenham, Norfolk
Printed and bound in Great Britain by The Cromwell Press Ltd

To the Risen Christ
who is unfailingly present as 'Body Given'

With Gratitude
for my Mother and Father
who reverenced the sacramental quality of created matter;
Pope John Paul II;
my Community, the Franciscan Sisters of the Eucharist;
and all who collaborate in developing a Theology of the Body.

Contents

Introduction

EVERY mystery of Christian faith touches upon the meaning of human embodiment. 'In fact,' says Benedict Ashley, 'any question I know how to ask concerns bodies, since even if something exists that is not bodily, I will know it only if somehow it contacts me as I am a body. Therefore, the puzzle of my body-self is a *universal* question, conditioning every other question I may ask.'[1] Why, then, has it taken almost two thousand years for Theology of the Body to be recognized as a distinct theological discipline? While the answer to that is complex, it is a Christian axiom that the capacity to receive and to understand revealed truths more deeply comes only when there is a 'fullness of time.'

In that light, it is not surprising that a distinct Theology of the Body would only emerge in the latter half of the twentieth century, when the possibilities of human embodiment and matter were opened in ways that former generations could not have foreseen. Since faith and the theological search to understand faith are always operative within a cumulative history, they benefit from every human advance in penetrating the truths of creation, and they are challenged by all that threatens to distort what has been received as revealed. Sometimes it is the latter that opens theological search to greater depths. Theological breakthroughs often bear the mark of historical events. St. Augustine, for example, was impelled to write *The City of God* when barbarian forces threatened Western civilization. Now, at the threshold of the third millennium of Christianity, when the body-person has become humanity's chief artifact, there is a new urgency to search the meaning of embodiment. Since the 1960s a number of works have been written concerning body-centered

[1] Benedict Ashley, *Theologies of the Body: Humanist and Christian* (Braintree, MA, 1985), p. 4.

issues, but the leading advocate for the development of Body Theology has been Pope John Paul II, who began to lay a foundation for it in his weekly Audiences of 1978, and continues to build on that foundation in the writings and addresses that span his Pontificate.

Although it is a newly-emerging discipline, Theology of the Body encompasses a vast and constantly expanding field of study. This book, as indicated by the initial word *Toward* in the title, is intended to serve as a basic text and entry-point for those whose 'faith seeks understanding' concerning the body: 1) it places basic questions to be pondered concerning the meaning and destiny of the lived body and the material universe; 2) it explores reasons for the ambivalence (at times the mistrust and hostility) that Christians have experienced in regard to the human body; 3) it locates the *meaning* of embodiment within the core revealed mysteries of Christian faith; and 4) it relates this meaning to concrete historical experience.

From the outset it is important to point out several methodological choices made in preparing this book. The first concerns terminology. The reader needs to be aware that a certain ambiguity attends the use of the terms 'body' and 'flesh.' Across the centuries these words have accumulated multifaceted meanings. Their use in philosophical and theological discourse is complicated by the fact that they touch so immediately upon subjective identity and experience. Their theological use is not a novel challenge, however. From earliest Christian reflection upon the faith, it was necessary to take words of everyday coinage within the Greek-speaking world and designate how they were intended within theological discourse. For example, the early Fathers chose words such as *sarx* (flesh), *logos* (Word), and *hypostasis* (individual being) to express aspects of the most profound mysteries of Christian faith.

In the present age also there is the need to use common words such as 'body' and 'flesh' in theological reflection, but to clarify their meaning within a developing Theology of the Body. As Arthur Vogel has noted, our bodies locate and center our experience, and '. . . body relations or the extension of those relations in language are the only means by which we can begin to know persons in the world. The Christian God who wanted human beings to know him as a person became incarnate – took a body

– for that very reason.'[2] Further, says Vogel, 'The recognition of personal presence begins with bodies,'[3] so that any religious theology concerning a personal God, or any knowledge of God that is significant for daily life must of necessity be a Body Theology.

For that reason, all theological terms employed in this book regarding human embodiment are to be understood within the context of the whole *person*. Unless the context specifies otherwise, 'body,' 'flesh,' 'the lived (or living) body,' 'the incarnate human being,' 'the embodied self,' and 'body-person' refer to the whole living human being, expressed bodily in the world, and these terms will be used interchangeably as appropriate. The search for adequate terminology to express the whole human person enfleshed in the world is ongoing, among philosophers as well as theologians.[4] As will be seen in subsequent chapters, to reflect theologically upon the embodied person is to penetrate ever more deeply, in the light of Revelation and Tradition, into the sacred mystery of the total person from the perspective of corporeality.

Second, it is necessary to note briefly the importance of *interdisciplinary insights* in the development of a contemporary Theology of the Body. As noted earlier, theological tasks are always carried out within a given moment of history. Whatever allows deeper understanding of the truths of creation assists the theological task of 'seeking understanding' regarding matters of faith. Any science or discipline (theoretical or applied) which offers a deeper glimpse into truth is indirectly collaborating in the theological task. This is especially the case in regard to Theology of the Body, which benefits from the work of those who minutely probe the processes of the living human body, and confirm their relationship with the rest of the material universe. Such findings are utilized in this book whenever they are deemed helpful.

This points to a third methodological choice in this work: to

---

[2] Arthur Vogel, *Body Theology: God's Presence in Man's World* (New York, 1973), p. ix.
[3] Arthur Vogel, *Body Theology*, p. ix.
[4] Richard Zaner, for example explores terms such as 'my body *qua* mine' (G. Marcel); and 'body-proper' (M. Merleau-Ponty) in *The Problem of Embodiment: Some Contributions to a Phenomenology of the Body*, 2nd ed. (The Hague, 1971), especially pp. 14–43, 152.

reflect on the body *relationally* as understood within the hierarchy of the truths of Christian faith: from the Trinity and the Incarnation, through creation. To narrow that perspective would mean the loss of authentic understanding of embodiment. While it is essential to focus now on one particular aspect of embodiment and then on another, this must always be done relationally – ultimately in reference to those trinitarian *relations* that are Personal, and which are imaged in the human body-person as well as found vestigially in all creation. In the following chapters it will be shown how the very *meaning* of human existence is the vocation to become an embodied self-gift in image of the relational inner life of the Trinity. In his article 'Concerning the Notion of Person in Theology,' for example, Cardinal Joseph Ratzinger writes of the relational meaning of trinitarian Persons in a manner that cryptically illumines the meaning of human embodied 'person' within the material universe:

> One could thus define the first person as self-donation in fruitful knowledge and love; it is not the one who gives himself, in whom the act of self-donation is found, but it is this self-donation, pure reality of act. An idea that appeared again in our century in modern physics is here anticipated: that there is pure act-being. We know that in our century the attempt has been made to reduce matter to a wave, to a pure act of streaming. What may be a questionable idea in the context of physics was asserted by theology in the fourth and fifth century about the persons in God, namely, that they are nothing but the act of relativity toward each other.[5]

A fourth aspect of method employed in this book flows from the interdisciplinary and relational characteristics just described. It is the use of analogical language. As Ratzinger's compact statement shows, it is possible to find analogies to intimate trinitarian life in the research findings of contemporary physics, and, in turn, to relate them to theological assertions of the Fathers of the Church! The Fathers themselves made frequent use of analogy, as St. Paul had done before them.

An analogy expresses a direct comparison between persons or

[5] Cardinal Joseph Ratzinger, 'Concerning the Notion of Person in Theology,' *Communio*, XVII (Fall, 1990), p. 444.

things, and suggests a resemblance in at least one of their attributes or circumstances or effects. Because the Roman Catholic tradition sees no opposition between nature and grace, Catholic theology has recognized a harmony between two major kinds of analogies: a) *analogia entis* (analogy of being) which basically consists in taking concepts drawn from natural knowledge and applying them to God; and b) *analogia fidei* (analogy of faith) which refers to God's use of human concepts in divine revelation. The universal *Catechism of the Catholic Church* acknowledges both types of analogy. In regard to the analogy of being, the *Catechism* affirms that a 'corresponding perception of their Creator' can be found in the beauty and greatness of creatures. Although *all* creatures have 'a certain resemblance to God' and reflect God's infinite perfection in their finite truth, goodness and beauty, human beings are distinctly created in God's image and likeness.[6] The writers of the *Catechism* stressed the analogy of faith in a particular manner, urging '*Be attentive to the analogy of faith*. By "analogy of faith" we mean the coherence of the truths of faith among themselves and within the whole plan of Revelation.'[7]

Analogies allow the perception of difference and likeness. Because they provide a way of seeing at least some likeness between what is known and what is still basically unknown (or imperfectly known) they assist those whose faith seeks understanding: a) to perceive more readily the coherence of the truths of faith; and b) to integrate into the context of faith whatever insight of truth is received. Such analogies may come through scientific observation, through ordinary life experiences, or through the human capacity to perceive relationships.

The use of metaphor, simile and parable is a way of extending analogical thinking. These prove especially helpful in expanding theological search into essentially fresh avenues. As will be concretely shown later, Christ made use of varied forms of comparison when he imparted to his first followers the essentials of the profound Revelation that he had come to impart through his own presence, words and actions. In order to prepare them for at least an elementary capacity to receive the mysterious, unim-

---

[6] See *Catechism of the Catholic Church* (Libreria Editrice Vaticana, 1994), #41.
[7] *Catechism*, #114.

agined Self-gift of inner trinitarian life which he brought incarnately to them, he selected from their familiar world what could serve as entry-points of comparison. Ultimately, all that is good, true and beautiful bears some vestige of trinitarian life. It appears, says Battista Mondin, that all theological concepts originate by way of analogy.

> In fact, when God talks to man, He does not make use of concepts entirely new but of concepts (and appropriate linguistic symbols) that are already familiar to man. So, for instance, He says to man that God is *father, creator, judge,* etc. i.e. He makes use of concepts that man already has. But in doing this God expects man and helps him to reshape his old concepts in order to adapt them to the new meaning, for the concepts of father, creator, judge, etc., cannot be attributed to God with the same meaning which they have when applied to human beings.[8]

In a particular manner, analogy assists in the theological exploration of embodiment and the material universe, since the task requires bringing diverse – sometimes, seemingly incompatible – insights into relationship. At times the juxtaposition of persons, events and physical realities passes into faith reflection by way of humor. In the conclusion of his book, *The Office of Peter and the Structure of the Church*, for example, Hans Urs von Balthasar wrote that the figure of Peter 'is an impossibility, made possible only by the will of the One who created him.' He continues:

> A fisherman from Galilee is planted at the center of the Empire, inherits it by being killed by it – but he is not killed as his Lord was, whom he betrayed. He is crucified upside down, with his feet uppermost, to make amends for his betrayal. It is too sublime: it is positively grotesque.
>
> Like Sancho Panza and Don Quixote, Simon Peter and Christ form a constellation.[9]

While the task of this book is to provide an introductory reflection on human embodiment within the coherence of the

[8] Battista Mondin, *The Principle of Analogy in Protestant and Catholic Theology,* 2nd rev. ed. (The Hague, 1968), p. 185.
[9] Hans Urs von Balthasar, *The Office of Peter and the Structure of the Church,* trans. Andree Emery (San Francisco, 1986), p. 356.

truths of faith, the *historical experiences of embodiment within the first two Christian millennia reflect inconsistencies that lead one to echo Balthasar's observation regarding Peter.* The vocation to be an embodied image of the divine Creator has often seemed an impossibility, made possible only by the will of the Creator. Thus, the first chapter of this book on the Theology of the Body begins with a brief historical survey of the Christian struggle to come to an authentic understanding of the body. The ultimate self-revelation of God in Jesus Christ did not settle the difficulties of receiving and understanding the mysteries of faith. Christian Revelation is fully accomplished in Christ Risen, who, with the Father, in the Holy Spirit, is perpetually given in covenantal Self-gift in his body and blood. To enter that mystery of faith more deeply is the sacred task of Body Theology.

I

The Body in Christian History

SINCE the history of Christian *experience* is rife with contradictions regarding the human body, it is important, prior to introducing a contemporary Theology of the Body, to show briefly why there have been dramatic fluctuations in understanding matter and human embodiment, and how these have impacted on Christian life. To begin with, a clear distinction needs to be made between official Church *doctrine* (the authentic, developing clarification of revealed truths), and *theology* (the ongoing effort to understand and apply the revealed truths of faith within any given period of history). Theological inquiry (the attempt to understand faith and to perceive its implications) can, at times, result in distortions that touch upon enduring core doctrines. Further, Christian life is always immersed in history, and is necessarily marked by philosophical, social, and political influences, as well as those of a more inexplicable nature such as taboos and fears. While it is impossible to detail these influences here, they need to be described briefly because they have often gravely affected Christian attitudes toward embodiment. Otherwise, it would be difficult to comprehend how Christian theology and praxis, despite their grounding in body-involving mysteries, have succumbed at times to serious distortions.

The roots of incarnational faith are evident in the New Testament writings which affirm that Christianity, from its inception, was closely identified with specific claims concerning the body: that the Word, the Second Person of the Trinity was conceived in the womb of the Virgin Mary; that after his birth the incarnate Son of God lived as 'the son of the carpenter' in Nazareth; that he revealed the divine economy of salvation not only in his spoken words and the outward 'signs' of his public ministry, but, above all, in his Self-gift in the body and blood.

When St. Paul wrote to the Corinthians (ca. AD 57), he assured them that his teaching concerning the reality of Christ's death and resurrection had not been of his own devising. It had been 'received.' He succinctly summarized the Paschal Event by saying: that Christ had truly died for our sins, that he had been buried, that he had been raised to life, and that he appeared to chosen witnesses (see 1 Cor. 15:3–8).[1] If that is not true, wrote Paul, then no one is raised from the dead; all who have died have simply perished and humanity is left in sin. Indeed, he pressed, if Christ has not truly risen, those who hope in him 'are the most unfortunate of all people' (1 Cor. 15:19). But Christ *has* risen said Paul. It was only with that firm assurance that he took up particular questions that the community at Corinth had raised concerning risen bodies.

In New Testament writings, the pivotal importance of embodiment is often made explicit through questions. Mary queries the archangel Gabriel concerning the possibility of her bearing Jesus in her body: 'But how can this come about, since I am a virgin?' (Lk. 1:34). She is assured that the power of the Holy Spirit will enable her to conceive the 'Son of the Most High' in her virginal womb. Subsequently, when Mary visits her cousin Elizabeth, the latter asks in amazement: 'Why should I be honoured with a visit from the mother of my Lord?' (Lk. 1:43). Within Elizabeth's womb, the unborn John leaps before the presence of Christ still unseen in Mary's womb. Gospel accounts of Jesus' public life are also punctuated by body-centered questions: 'Which of these is easier: to say to the paralytic, "Your sins are forgiven" or to say, "Get up, pick up your stretcher and walk"?' (Mk. 2:9). 'What sign will you give to show us that we should believe in you? What work will you do?' (Jn. 6:30). 'How can this man give us his flesh to eat?' (Jn. 6:52). Many disciples stopped following Jesus when he identified himself as the Bread of Life and revealed that his flesh was real food, his blood real drink. This revelation concerning his own Self-gift was so decisive that he turned to the Twelve and asked: ' What about you, do you want to go away, too?' (Jn. 6:67).

Every mystery of Christian faith bears a body dimension, including the core revelations concerning inner trinitarian life, the Incarnation, and the Eucharist. These could only be made

---

[1] Unless indicated otherwise, citations from Scripture are from *The Jerusalem Bible*, ed. Alexander Jones *et al* (Garden City, NY, 1966).

known through Jesus Christ's embodied presence. In *Lumen Gentium*, the Dogmatic Constitution on the Church of Vatican Council II, the Eucharist is designated both 'the source and summit of the Christian life' (#11). The universal *Catechism of the Catholic Church*, dwelling on the reason for this centrality of the Eucharist in the life of the Church, states:

> The mode of Christ's presence under the Eucharistic species is unique. It raises the Eucharist above all the sacraments as 'the perfection of the spiritual life and the end to which all the sacraments tend.' In the most blessed sacrament of the Eucharist 'the body and blood, together with the soul and divinity, of our Lord Jesus Christ and, therefore, *the whole Christ is truly, really and substantially* contained.' 'This presence is called "real" – by which is not intended to exclude the other types of presence as if they could not be "real" too, but because it is presence in the fullest sense: that is to say, it is a *substantial* presence by which Christ, God and man, makes himself wholly and entirely present.'[2]

In the New Testament, particularly in the writings of St. Paul, the Church itself is explicitly described in bodily terms. Paul writes: 'Now you together are Christ's body; but each of you is a different part of it' (1 Cor. 12:27).[3] In continuity with the New Testament and Christian faith through the centuries, the Second Vatican Council says of Christ's followers, drawn from every nation, that they constitute a *mystical body*.[4]

IDENTIFYING MAJOR REASONS FOR DISTORTIONS

Why, then, have many Christians at times been persuaded to consider the body to be unworthy, suspect, or even vile? The reasons are numerous and diverse, but it is important to cite at least eight: 1) taboos, resulting from fear of the unknown; 2)

---

[2] *Catechism*, #1374. Quotations included in this text, in sequence, are from St. Thomas Aquinas, *STh* III, 73, 3c; Council of Trent (1551): DS 1651; and Paul VI, *Mysterium Fidei*, 39.
[3] See also 1 Cor. 12:12–30; Rom. 12:4; Eph. 2:16, 4:4, 5:30; and Col. 1:18.
[4] See *Lumen Gentium*, #7.

ignorance concerning human procreation and 'women's mysteries'; 3) various forms of dualism; 4) the impact of the barbarian invasions; 5) the revival in the high Middle Ages of Aristotle's erroneous theories concerning procreation, female bodies and male-female relationships; 6) abuses of sacraments and sacramentals prior to the Reformation and the ensuing backlash; 7) the new dualism of the Enlightenment; and 8) the technological revolution of the twentieth century, in which the human body has become a major artifact. Each of these must be acknowledged briefly as contributing to distorted notions of the human body and the material universe.

Taboos and Unreasonable Fears

First to be considered then are *taboos*, which stem from heightened fear of the unknown or from fear of something perceived as dangerous but beyond ordinary control. Persons who are constrained by taboos attempt to isolate or contain what proves threatening, to placate mysterious forces which exceed their control, and to create rituals which will consistently be effective in preventing harm. Some of the most fundamental taboos have been those which concern the body, especially those which are associated with blood and what can be termed 'women's mysteries': menstruation, gestation, birth and lactation.

Long before the Christian era, 'The Great Goddess' of fertility was a focus of worship. Archeologists have found numerous images of her from the Mediterranean basin to the Russian steppes and the Indus valley. They range from the 'Venus of Willendorf' with her pendulous breasts and enormous thighs and buttocks (found in Austria, dated ca. 30,000 BC) to slender, asthenic figurines. Despite their abundance and variety, they accent aspects of a woman's body and many are ochre-stained. Wolfgang Lederer writes:

> Some are standing or sitting, some simply squatting or lying down, some squatting to give birth – to a child, or, perhaps, to an animal.... They share the emphasis on breasts and pubic zone, often with strong accentuation of the vulva, as perhaps it might appear in childbirth or in aroused tumescence.[5]

[5] Wolfgang Lederer, *The Fear of Women* (New York, 1968), p. 10.

Frequently such images have no feet since they 'emerged' from the earth, indeed *were* the earth. They were often venerated in caves or recessed areas, but even today, in the sun-bleached ruins of Ostia, the old port of Rome, one finds among the weeds portions of elaborate mosaics that clearly belong to an area of Ostia once designated for worship of the Great Mother.

Why such extensive veneration of the goddess? For primitive peoples, there was a strong association of the earth, the moon (Mother Earth and the Moon Mother were one) and the bodies of women. Mysterious, dangerous powers were at work among them. In the cyclic, life-giving powers of women's bodies, ancient peoples found a correspondence to the moon's phases and they thought it necessary to placate the goddess of fertility so that she might be favorable to them. Women's menstruation and their child-bearing phases were surrounded by taboos since the mysterious powers of women, earth and moon could result in either life or death. Taboos varied, but in many tribes, menstruation ('moon-change') often required a woman's complete isolation and no man could approach her. Whatever a menstruating woman touched was harmed to the extent that, in some tribes, a menstruant could not even touch her *own* head to alleviate an itch. She would be given a stick for that purpose! For some tribes, a menstruant's *shadow* could contaminate. Esther Harding points out that her touch could harm not only the immediate food concerned, but the entire tribal food supply:

> The evil effects of her touch reach beyond the realm of food: sickness and disaster of all kinds may be caused by a chance encounter with her. For these reasons women are required to seclude themselves most strictly during their 'dangerous' periods and to exercise the greatest caution in their contact with the outside world.... For it is believed that if a man 'looks upon a menstruating woman his bones will soften, he will lose his manhood,' will even die, while his weapons and implements will become useless, his nets will no longer catch fish, and his arrows will not kill deer.[6]

[6] Esther Harding, *Woman's Mysteries: Ancient and Modern* (New York, 1971), pp. 57–58.

In Leviticus 15 there are strict regulations concerning a woman's ritual uncleanness during menstruation. Israel's laws concerning 'uncleanness,' extended much further, however. Bodily emissions of both sexes caused uncleanness, as did sexual intercourse, childbirth, contact with a corpse, and touching a leper. From the Gospels, it is apparent that Jesus during the course of his earthly life transcended the notion of 'uncleanness.' In his relations with women, he was not deterred by taboos, customs or laws. Perhaps the most dramatic example of this is found in John 4, which tells of Jesus' encounter with a Samaritan woman. At the common well, he initiated conversation with her, which was a departure from the norm not only because she was a woman, but also because she was a member of a 'despised race.' He took no precautions, however, and requested that she give him a drink from her own vessel. To drink from a woman's vessel was to risk contact with her spittle. If she would have been menstruating, there was a severe taboo involved. David Daube notes: 'The woman Jesus met was deemed unclean, like a menstruant, and her uncleanness was conveyed to the vessel she held. . . . If it was a vessel from which she used to drink, the case was particularly serious: the spittle of a menstruant was contaminating in a very high degree.'[7]

The Gospels indicate that Jesus was free of any restrictions concerning 'women's mysteries.' Women accompanied him on his journeys and supplied for his needs and those of the apostolic band. Jesus' parables are salted with examples drawn from the common experiences of both men and women. Nevertheless, in ensuing centuries, what was transmitted through folk customs and cultural mores bore great power, and the daily life of Christians reflected this. According to Isidore of Seville (ca. 636), for example, if an 'unclean' woman touched fruit, it would not ripen and the plant would die. In Bede's *Ecclesiastical History* 1:27, it is recorded that St. Augustine of Canterbury sought the advice of Pope St. Gregory I (AD 601) on the following matters: might a pregnant woman be baptized? may a menstruant enter the church and receive communion? how long should a new mother refrain from entering the church after childbirth? Gregory's answers

---

[7] David Daube, *The New Testament and Rabbinic Judaism* (London, 1965), p. 374.

affirmed the naturalness of these bodily conditions and said that they did not prevent a woman from full participation in the life of the Church. Nevertheless, he observed that menstruation was an 'infirmity' that afflicted women 'because of their nature' and it was something they suffered 'unwillingly.'[8] Joan Morris cites penitential guidebooks of the eighth to eleventh centuries that still restricted women, including nuns, from entering a church or communicating during their periods.[9] It would be simplistic to isolate these examples from the total range of influences which characterize male-female relationships. The intent here is simply to indicate the powerful effect that bodily processes, especially those relating to sexuality and fertility, have on human thought and behavior. As will be seen in later chapters, the living body is inherently mysterious and sacred. These very qualities can make individuals and societies vulnerable to fears and taboos.

Early Forms of Dualism

Like taboos, *dualism* in its varied forms seemed to provide ways of coping with the anxieties and tensions that characterize embodied life in a material universe. *Unlike* taboos, early systems of dualism were sometimes supported by elaborate philosophical theories and carried a sophisticated appeal. The very word 'dualism' indicates division into two separate entities. More specifically, it refers here to the antagonistic division between 'body' and 'soul,' between 'the material' and 'the spiritual.' Christianity emerged at a time when two basically different concepts of the human person were found in societies surrounding the Mediterranean: the Greek concept, a 'more (Plato) or less (Aristotle) extreme dualism,'[10] and the Hebrew concept which presumed the

---

[8] For further elaboration on the impact of menstruation and women's embodiment in Christian history, see Harding, *Women's Mysteries;* and Sister M. Timothy Prokes, *The Flesh Was Made Word* (Doctoral dissertation, University of St. Michael's College, Toronto, 1976), especially pp. 30–120.
[9] See Joan Morris, *The Lady Was a Bishop: The Hidden Story of Women with Clerical Ordination and the Jurisdiction of Bishops* (New York, 1973), p. 111.
[10] Karl Rahner and Herbert Vorgrimler, *Theological Dictionary*, ed. Cornelius Ernst, trans. Richard Strachan (New York, 1965), p. 59.

unity of the body-person.[11] Just as New Testament writings strongly affirm the goodness of the body and the material universe, they also provide evidence that the early Church was already involved in a struggle with dualistic influences.

The term 'Gnosticism,' derived from *gnosis* the Greek word for knowledge, encompassed a variety of dualistic movements which became especially problematic in the opening centuries of Christianity. For Gnostics, *knowledge*, and it alone, was redemptive. Their spiritual leaders taught that the universe itself was the result of a fallen condition, and that the body was useless, deceptive compared to the spirit hidden within it. Through philosophical knowledge, coupled with rejection of the material world, Gnostics hoped to take flight to the divine. They followed a path of asceticism that distorted the meaning of the body, sexuality and male-female relationships.

Peter Brown describes in some detail how Valentinus, a Christian spiritual guide in second century Rome, utilized mythical systems in which there was an antagonistic polarity not only between matter and spirit, but also between male and female. The myth of the fall, repentance and return of Sophia, for example, allowed Valentinus to adapt the marital imagery of his time. In the myth, Sophia, or the principle of divine Wisdom (which once resided in the *pleroma* as a mighty force in a *completely spiritual universe*) desired to have God's divine self-knowledge. Incapable of achieving this, Sophia rebelled, and in her despair at being separated from God, created the material world as 'an abortive attempt to imitate an infinitely distant, invisible, and ever-elusive model. The world created by Sophia spoke only of the chasm that separated what was from what should be.'[12] While Christ was considered to have brought Sophia's rebellion

[11] The first disciples shared a Jewish heritage which included the assumption that a human being is a single psychosomatic unity of two elements. When the Hebrews wished to emphasize what might be termed the life-force, the breath, or the center of the human personality they used the term *nephesh*. When they wished to indicate the whole living being in its concrete, fleshly aspects, they used the term *basar*. There was no pejorative connotation in their use of *basar*, which is usually translated as 'body' or 'flesh.' As Frank Bottomley observes, words such as 'heart,' 'glory,' 'soul' and 'flesh' corresponded to different manifestations of the whole living person. See his *Attitudes to the Body in Western Christendom* (London, 1979), p. 17.
[12] Peter Brown, *The Body and Society: Men, Women, and Sexual Renunciation in Early Christianity* (New York, 1988), p. 108.

to a halt, he certainly did not achieve this through bodily self-gift. Rather, in the mythological system of polarities, matter was viewed as an ephemeral accident, a tragic dislocation from perfect spirituality. Brown says of Valentinus' teachings:

> Precisely because his view of the physical world was so bleak, Valentinus offered his Christian charges a hope of redemption that was more drastic than that of any of his pagan contemporaries. The physical universe would not remain eternally harmonious, schooled by the gentle play of the spirit. It was a mistake that must be rectified. Parts of the universe, the human body among them, would eventually be cast off as abortive and misconceived creations. All that remained, however, would sink back into the spirit. The visible world would be swallowed up again into the perfect spiritual order from which it had flickered uneasily in a short moment of confusion.[13]

Gnostic spirituality, which assumed that material beings were intrinsically degenerate, had a radical effect on man-woman relationships and marriage. Gnostics were far from original in considering women to be inferior to men. That notion permeated the empire of the early Christian era, bolstered by erroneous theories concerning sexuality and procreation. Six hundred years earlier, Aristotle had taught that the conception of a female child was the result of some mishap. His certainty that males were superior to females corresponded with his explanation that all beings are composed of a union of 'form and matter.' Accordingly, in the act of procreation, the male seed is the 'form' which determines the indeterminate 'matter' provided by the female. If all goes well in the act of procreation, he said in *De generatione animalium*, a male will be conceived. The conception of a female, on the other hand, results from some imperfection: either there is a debility in the active power of the male seed, or there is some indisposition in the matter provided by the female. In fact, Aristotle conjectured, the conception of a female may even be the result of some extrinsic change such as a humid wind from the south. Because such assertions had become common currency, radical misunderstandings followed concerning matter, the human body, and woman-man relations.

[13] Peter Brown, *The Body and Society*, p. 109.

Christian Gnostics, according to Brown, treasured Gospel accounts concerning Christ's relationships with women (especially Mary Magdalen) since they seemed to verify the belief that women were perpetually inferior, and that they were willingly, irresistibly absorbed into the male guiding principle.[14] The concluding logion of the apocryphal Gnostic *Gospel of Thomas* validated the Gnostic notion that 'redemption' would take place in two stages. First, the female would be given form by the male. Second, whatever was not 'spirit' would be absorbed. Thus, a female would be saved by becoming male. The logion claims:

> Simon Peter said to the Apostles: Let Mary depart from our midst, for women are not worthy of our life. Jesus answered: Behold, I will turn her into a male, so that she may become a living spirit as you men: every woman who has become a male will enter into the Kingdom of heaven.[15]

While there were varieties of Gnosticism, they shared several common elements. In addition to a systematized dualism, there was a rejection of the present time in its concreteness; a 'flight' to the divine through philosophical knowledge and ascetical practices; and a rejection of legal norms. Obviously, such beliefs and practices influenced the Gnostic attempts to understand and explain Christ. To begin with, it seemed impossible that the immortal Logos could actually become man and suffer. While *Docetism* (from a Greek word meaning 'to seem') was not a particular sect in itself, it was a christological opinion that Christ had only an *apparent* body. He only seemed to suffer and die. Were that so, St. Paul's instruction concerning the reality of Christ's death and resurrection would apply once more: if Christ had not become truly embodied, then he had not died or risen and Christians were only to be pitied because there had been no redemption from sin. 1 John, in its strong affirmation of the reality of Christ's body, is already a response to Docetic thought:

[14] See Peter Brown, *The Body and Society*, p. 113.
[15] Trans. by Dom Wulstan Hibberd in Jacques Hervieux, *The New Testament Apocrypha* (New York, 1960), p. 150. For further explanation of Gnostic abolition of sexual distinctions in this Gnostic gospel, see R. M. Grant, *Gnosticism and Early Christianity*, 2nd ed. (New York, 1966), pp. 186–189.

Something which has existed since the beginning,
that we have heard,
and we have seen with our own eyes;
that we have watched
and touched with our hands:
the Word, who is life –
this is our subject.
That life was made visible:
we saw it and we are giving our testimony,
telling you of the eternal life
which was with the Father and has been made visible to us.
What we have seen and heard
we are telling you
so that you too may be in union with us... (1 Jn. 1:1–3)

While Docetists claimed that the flesh was unsuitable for Christ, *Encratists* rejected marriage and considered sexual behavior evil (their name derives from the Greek word *enkrateia* – continence). Encratites placed emphasis on the account of Adam and Eve's fall, interpreting it to mean that humans had abandoned their marriage to God's Spirit and were now forced to have sexual relations with one another, something that had not been in God's original plan. Human sexual intercourse resulted in a blurring of the boundaries between animal and human life. Some followers of Tatian thought that the loss of the Spirit was directly caused by a sexual act.[16] Following the fall, sexuality, marriage and death were part of the same cycle. Thus, Encratites refrained from sexual intercourse and marriage, but increased their own ranks through adoptions. They were recognized not only by their communal celibacy, but also by their abstinence from meat and wine.

The Women's Movement of the twentieth century has found an interest in Encratist literature since it emphasized the difficulties and immense pressures that society exerted upon married women in regard to their bodies:

> In the Encratite tradition, the end of the present age was to be brought about by the boycott of the womb. And the boycott of the womb was crucial because sexuality was presented less as a

---

[16] See Peter Brown, *The Body and Society*, p. 93.

drive than as the symbol of ineluctable processes, the clearest token of human bondage. . . . Seen from the woman's viewpoint, the change from virginity to childbearing revealed most blatantly the chasm that separated eternity from a humanity now caught in the cruel flux of time.[17]

The third century Babylonian, Mani, offered yet another variation of Gnosticism. His approach was 'mixed,' however. His followers, those who belonged to the 'Church of the Mind,' were to reach the realm of light by accepting his teachings, attaining self-knowledge, and practicing strict asceticism. While the human body generally was considered vile, the bodies of the Manichean 'Elect' were thought to be sun and moon come down to earth. The Elect's cultic meals (served by their catechumens) passed through their holy bodies in a process of distillation that set free the 'light' trapped in fruits and vegetables and liberated souls from matter. A close connection was established between food and sexuality. The Elect refrained from sexual intercourse, but if sexual desire stirred in them, it was thought to derive from a remissness in diet. The ordinary *auditors*, unlike the Elect, were married. They were sexually abstinent for fifty days a year, fasted, and looked forward to being set free with the Elect.

It is not surprising that the writings of the Fathers of the Church bear marks of these and other anti-body, anti-matter movements. While many wrote precisely to defend the Christian faith against errors concerning Christ's real enfleshment, and the goodness of body and creation, they often betrayed their own struggle to maintain a stance consistent with the faith they so vigorously professed. St. Augustine, whose early life was steeped in Platonism, and who followed the teachings of Mani for nine years, exemplifies this. Late twentieth-century studies concerning embodiment, sexuality and woman-man relationships often include citations from Church Fathers such as St. Jerome, Tertullian, St. John Chrysostom and St. Augustine in order to demonstrate their distorted views concerning the body, sexuality and marriage. There is no doubt that their writings reveal an ambivalence concerning the body; *this was part of their struggle, from within the limitations of their own historical moment, to under-*

---

[17] Peter Brown, *The Body and Society*, p. 99.

stand and explicate what had been given through Revelation in Jesus Christ.

Celibacy for the sake of the Kingdom was already recognized in New Testament writings, and Jesus clearly affirmed the goodness of marriage; yet it has taken centuries of struggle and development to understand more fully the *integrated meaning* of sexuality, celibacy and marriage that was revealed in Jesus Christ. Insight has often come through the correction of abuses and exaggerations of both a theoretical and a practical nature. It would be anachronistic to expect that what has been slowly, often painfully learned over almost two millennia, should have been readily apparent in the early centuries of the Church. As appropriate, points of ambivalence in patristic writings will be cited in later chapters in relation to the development of Theology of the Body. While some of the Fathers wrote from a profound appreciation of the spiritual meaning of celibacy and marriage, they too, wrote from within the limitations of their moment in history.

Until Constantine lifted the ban on Christian life and worship in the fourth century, sporadic periods of persecution made the profession of Christian faith demanding to the point of martyrdom. Christians considered the bodies of saints torn by beasts or set afire to light an emperor's garden party to be sacred relics. Not only did they reverently gather the martyrs' remains for burial; they also celebrated Eucharist over their graves. Some had been martyred specifically because they would not violate their promise of celibacy for the sake of the Kingdom. When official persecutions ceased and Constantine overtly supported Christianity, martyrdom also ceased to be a major way of demonstrating total dedication to the faith. As a result, many sought an alternative in strict asceticism. There was a 'move to the desert' that paralleled in time the later Gnostic and Manichean cults. Accounts of the desert-dwellers not only tell of severe asceticism, but also of what may seem to contemporary readers a disproportionate number of sexual struggles and fantasies. As Peter Brown points out, it was a time of deepening insight; despite the ascetics' heroics in attempting to escape carnality, desert life itself revealed the 'inextricable interdependence of body and soul.'[18]

---

[18] Peter Brown, *The Body and Society*, p. 236.

We can appreciate why sexuality proved such a strong force among the finest exponents of desert life, says Brown, since a monk's struggle with sexual fantasies was intimately interwoven with his state of soul. It wasn't that men such as Cassian, Dorotheos of Gaza and John Climacus were more fearful of being tempted sexually than in other ways:

> It was rather that the body, in which sexuality lurked with such baffling tenacity, had come to be viewed in the searching light of a new, high hope: 'What is this mystery in me? What is the purpose of this mixture of body and soul? How can I be my own friend and my own enemy?' Yet everyone, John insists, 'should struggle to raise his clay, so to speak, to a place on the throne of God.'[19]

From Barbarian Violence to Aristotelian Revival

The esteemed, self-imposed severity of the desert ascetics was soon eclipsed by the severity of the 'barbarian invasions.' For almost a millennium, what had been the Eastern-Western Empire was ravaged by wave after wave of invading forces. At first these were numerous warring 'barbarian' tribes that later would form the nations of Europe and Western Asia. When Europe had congealed into numerous fiefdoms and centers of economic exchange, there was a turnabout to the East, with waves of crusaders attempting to secure the embattled Christian East against the followers of Islam. For centuries, then, theological reflection on the 'mysterious mix of body and soul' was radically curtailed by the sheer need to survive and to protect one's domain. 'Penitentials' written for the guidance of confessors (who also often served as local judges) witness to the starkness and violence of ordinary life. Monasteries, in particular those based on Benedict's Rule, offered a balance of prayer, work and study, where nuns and monks not only salvaged what they could of Western civilization, but also taught and wrote, preparing the way for a resurgence of theological reflection and artistic expression in the later Middle Ages. Monastic achievement of creative insight regarding embodiment and male-female relationships reached an apex in the writings of Hildegard of Bingen

[19] Peter Brown, *The Body and Society*, p. 239.

(1098–1179). While she knew and utilized aspects of Aristotle's thought, she was able to break out of thought patterns which assumed the superiority of males. Francis Martin says that while her framework remains basically Aristotelian, Hildegard's observations 'consist mostly in a very insightful understanding into what we would call the psychosomatic typology of men and women. In this she is almost a phenomenologist before her time. She concludes that in the resurrection all will rise in the integrity of their bodies and their sex.'[20]

In the twelfth and thirteenth centuries there emerged a new appreciation for the body and for woman-man relationships. After a surfeit of violence came 'courtly love' in which knightly valor in combat was linked with self-sacrifice for the sake of an idealized love. The legends, poetry, art and song of the period celebrate the body and the good things of earth, as well as the transcendent qualities of faithful love and friendship. Regrettably, however, by the thirteenth century, when the major thrust of Western theological scholarship moved from the monasteries to the newly-founded universities, there was a dramatic separation between the shared scholarly work of women and men, since women were not permitted to teach or to enroll in the universities. For nearly seven centuries, this basic separation of the scholarly insights of men and women vitiated a balanced advance in the understanding of the lived body and the material universe. Further, this separation was accompanied by a perpetuation of erroneous teachings regarding procreation and the respective worth of male and female.

Thomas Aquinas drew heavily upon Aristotle's philosophical system when he formulated his synthesis of the faith in the thirteenth century. In a positive vein, Thomas rejected Platonic dualism and its disdain of the body, accepting Aristotle's theory of hylomorphism, which affirmed body-soul unity. On the one hand, he held that there is no existence of soul apart from existence of the body.[21] It is the nature of the soul, he said, to be the 'form' of the body (Ia. 90, 4, *ad* 1). On the other hand, Thomas said, it is the intellective principle that determines 'man'

---

[20] Francis Martin, *The Feminist Question: Feminist Theology in the Light of Christian Tradition* (Grand Rapids, MI, 1994), p. 369.
[21] See Thomas Aquinas, *Summa Theologiae*, Ia. 76, 7, *ad* 3. Further citations will be indicated within the text.

as a species, and while the body has no part in the operation of the intellect (Ia. 118, 2, *resp.*), the soul has sensory powers which require it to be joined to a body. Thomas exceeded Averroes' interpretation of Aristotle in maintaining that the soul was a substance in its own right (and did not die with the body). From our present understandings of personal wholeness, however, it is evident that he over-emphasized the 'intellectual.' Anton Pegis' succinct summary of Thomas' thought on body-soul unity as 'diminished intellectuality' is pertinent here:

> We cannot explain the soul by the body; we must explain the body by the soul.... The answer to the unity of man's nature lies in the soul, in the soul it lies in the intellect, and in the intellect it lies in the fact that, by itself, the human intellect is not the complete intellectual power of the intellectual substance that the soul is. Hence arises the notion of an intellect incarnated in the senses in order to be adequately an intellect; hence also the notion of soul and body as forming together an intellectual substance wholly intellectual, but of diminished intellectuality.[22]

Such a perspective not only 'intellectualizes' the body; it offers an interpretation of the actual human condition of embodiment as a 'diminishment' of the soul's capacity. Unlike Hildegard, Thomas assumed that Aristotle's theories concerning human procreation were to be received without question. He repeated the philosopher's teachings on the inferiority of females, described above. In his view, a woman is subservient in procreation, providing only passive matter to be 'formed' by the male seed. Further, Thomas explicitly rejected the body's participation in being in God's image (Ia. 3, 1, *ad* 2) since he held that the imaging of God pertains only to the mind (Ia. 93, 6, *sed contra*). Consonant with that conviction he taught that both men and women could be the image of God, since the mind had no sex (Ia. 93, 6, *ad* 2). But even here, in a secondary sense, a female could not image God to the extent that a male could. Man is the beginning and end of woman, just as God is the beginning and end of all creation (Ia. 93, 4, *ad* 1).

Because there were significant unresolved struggles and misunderstandings concerning the body, sexuality and the respective

---

[22] Anton C. Pegis, 'St. Thomas and the Unity of Man,' in *Progress in Philosophy*, ed. James McWilliams (Milwaukee, 1955), pp. 169–171.

worth of women and men, it is not surprising that many centuries of Christian life and worship passed before marriage was definitively named among the sacraments; even then, questions persisted regarding the suitability of sexual intercourse for expressing sacramental life. Church traditions regarding marriage had developed slowly. Only in the late fourth century did a bishop or priest in the East bless those marrying, either at the wedding feast or on the day prior to their wedding. St. Augustine was the earliest (and only patristic) Christian author to write extensively of sexuality and marriage, and the only Church Father to speak of it in terms of a sacrament. Yet, as Joseph Martos says: ' . . . in the end he affirmed that marriage was good even though sex was not.'[23] In the eleventh century, there was a rediscovery of Augustine's writings on marriage as a *sacramentum*, in which he taught that marriage was both a sacred pledge between the spouses, and (in accordance with Ephesians 5) a sign of Christ's union with the Church. At the Council of Florence (1439) marriage was included in the listing of the seven sacraments, and Augustine's teaching on the goods of marriage was adopted, namely: 'the procreation and education of children, fidelity between the spouses, and the indissolubility of the sacramental bond.'[24]

Sacramental Abuse, Reform, and Rejection

It is impossible to summarize briefly the melange of attitudes toward the body in the Christian West during the later Middle Ages and the beginning of the 'Modern Age.' Several crucial events, however, have bearing on our survey: the bubonic plague, the abuse of relics and sacramental matter, and the rejection of many aspects of sacramental life among Christians who attempted to eliminate these abuses in life and worship.

Shortly after Christian scholarship flourished in the High Middle Ages, and Christian art had celebrated the body and creation within the praise of God, there came the terror of the bubonic plague. In the attempt to avoid swift death and gain control over a disease that eluded medicinal cures, many reverted

[23] Joseph Martos, *Doors to the Sacred: A Historical Introduction to Sacraments in the Catholic Church* (Garden City, NY, 1981), p. 416.
[24] Joseph Martos, *Doors to the Sacred*, p. 434.

to practices that combined magic with Christian sacramentals and rituals. Among them were groups of 'flagellants' who sought to appease God by moving from city to city, conducting public self-flagellation according to a strictly prescribed ritual. The entrance of a priest or a woman into their ritual circle would nullify the 'effectiveness' of the bloody penitential rite.

Taking advantage of the simple faith and devotion of the unlearned, unscrupulous clergy preyed upon them for financial gain. In times of violence, illness, or plague, many could be persuaded to believe the authenticity of whatever was put forward as a *relic*. By the sixteenth century it was common for cities to claim the bodies of particular saints in order to become a center of pilgrimage and to promote economic gain. When a holy person died, there would be a struggle to obtain all or part of the deceased's body so that a place of pilgrimage could be maintained. When pilgrims arrived, they required lodging, food, and artifacts to take home for veneration. In some instances, when renowned holy persons died, it was necessary to secret their bodies away before they would be violated by those struggling to obtain relics. On the cold rainy night when St. John of the Cross died, for example, people poured into his cell within an hour, kissing his hands and feet, seeking relics by snipping his hair, cutting pieces from clothing and bandages, and pulling out swabs soaked in pus. Someone bit off a toe of the saint. At his funeral the following day, a mob forced past the friars and tore off John's scapular and habit as well as parts of his ulcerated flesh.

There was a similarity between the abuse of relics and the selling of indulgences: both offered a distorted, but concrete, sacramental dimension. There was a ritual, for example, in 'purchasing' an indulgence. A sacrificial payment was made, and a document was issued verifying that temporal punishment had been remitted either for oneself or for a soul in purgatory. In attempting to correct such abuses, sixteenth-century Reformers chose to *eliminate* the very sacramental traditions that could be distorted in this manner. Relying exclusively on descriptions given in the Scriptures, the Reformers claimed that only Baptism and Holy Eucharist could be termed sacraments (or 'ordinances'). Since proclamation of the Word became central, church buildings were stripped of images and bodily involvement in sacramental life was curtailed. In the more extreme reforms, singing and dancing were banned, and the drinking of stimulating beverages prohibited. Indirectly, Christians of the sixteenth and seventeenth centuries contributed to the new dualism of the Enlightenment.

THE BODY AS OBJECT AND ARTIFACT

Psychiatrist Karl Stern has described René Descartes as the St. Augustine of the Age of Reason. Descartes' new dualism divided the universe in two: *res cogitans* (that which thinks but has no extension); and *res extensa* (that which is spatial but lacks psychic qualities). Scientific 'objectivity' has attempted since then to attain such a division between the observer and the observed, considering it the methodological basis for any exact science. Stern notes:

> Where it goes beyond that, however, it develops into a disastrous fallacy. For one thing, it implies a fearful estrangement. Just think of nature as nothing but a huge, vastly extended soul-less machine which you can take apart experimentally and analyze mathematically, which you can run – but with which you have lost all oneness![25]

Stern, in his study of Descartes and six other male shapers of Western thought from the Enlightenment to the present, provides a psychiatrist's observations on the ways in which each was distorted in some manner in his relationships with women. In Sartre the estrangement from woman extended in a dramatic way to his estrangement from all that is material. In his novel *Nausea*, Sartre conveys to the reader a sense of the entire world as disgusting. Taken together, plants, animals and people are perceived as 'an infinite, slightly disgusting mass, not enough to make you retch, but just enough to maintain a nauseous sensation.'[26] Writing in the 1960s, Karl Stern maintained that it is only in the twentieth century that the 'estrangement from matter and the maternal has reached a point of no return.'[27] While a St. Francis of Assisi could rejoice in the multiplicity of created

[25] Karl Stern, *The Flight From Woman* (New York, 1965), p. 76.
[26] Karl Stern, *Flight From Woman*, p. 126.
[27] Karl Stern, *Flight From Woman*, p. 140.

things, Sartre found a 'narcissism of barrenness' in the abundance of creation. Says Stern:

> What Sartre said about Baudelaire we may say about Sartre himself: [Nature] is something huge, lukewarm which penetrates everything. Of that warm dampness, of that abundance, he was in perfect horror. Prolific Nature, which produces one single model in millions of copies, was bound to hurt his love for the rare. He, too, could say: 'I love everything which one can never see twice.' By this he praises absolute sterility.[28]

The ever-expanding ability to objectivize, analyze and rearrange material reality has opened the material universe *and the human body* to enormous restructuring. In the twentieth century, for the first time, it has been possible to separate aspects of the material world into discrete, infinitesimally minute bits, which move at high speeds, but which behave unpredictably and which elude the human capacity to grasp. The scientific and technological ability to penetrate matter can either 1) divide and objectivize embodied persons into discrete, interchangeable parts; or 2) assist in spurring the development of doctrine regarding the body-person. As Ratzinger notes, the findings of contemporary physics regarding the smallest bits of matter resonate with theological assertions of the fourth and fifth centuries concerning the persons in God: 'We know that in our century the attempt has been made to reduce matter to a wave, to a pure act of streaming. ... In God, person is the pure relativity of being turned toward the other; it does not lie on the level of substance – the substance is *one* – but on the level of dialogical reality, of relativity toward the other.'[29] In terms of Scripture, a *person* is not a closed substance, 'but the phenomenon of complete relativity.'[30] While the perfection of this is only in God, *relation* illumines what it means to be a human person. Thus, says Ratzinger, there is a transition from doctrines about God to Christology and from Christology to anthropology. It can be added: the transition continues from a theological anthropology to a theological study of matter.

---

[28] Karl Stern, *Flight From Woman*, p. 141.
[29] Joseph Ratzinger, 'Concerning the Notion of Person in Theology,' p. 444.
[30] Joseph Ratzinger, 'Concerning the Notion of Person in Theology,' p. 445.

THE BODY AND DEVELOPMENT OF DOCTRINE

This chapter has indicated how diverse influences in the history of Christianity have brought about distortions in faith understandings of the body. It will be the task in the following chapters to see how these inadequate understandings impel the development of a Theology of the Body as Revelation penetrates more deeply into the lived experience of the Church. As the twentieth century draws to a close, there is a dramatic surge in theological insight concerning the lived body: the same historical moment that evidences an 'objective' pulverization of the body-person opens the possibility of understanding in new ways the human vocation to be a communion of body-persons in the image and likeness of God. It is a moment for development of doctrine concerning the significance of the human body and the material universe – and a new moment for the development of theological reflection upon doctrines concerning the body.

As Thomas Rausch points out, Roman Catholic understanding of authentic doctrinal development always implies 'a particular understanding of revelation,'[31] and while there is a propositional element involved, God's Revelation comes not in propositions but ultimately and fully in and through the person of Jesus Christ. Doctrines are human expressions (authorized by the Church); they are the Church's attempt to formulate in human language what are divine mysteries grasped through faith. As such, they are conditioned and limited by the knowledge, vocabulary and conceptual frameworks available at a given moment of history. In the incorporation of new insights, whether these come from promptings of the Holy Spirit, or from cultural or scholarly developments, it may be necessary to reinterpret or understand an already defined doctrine within a new context, *without contradicting what has already been defined*. Development in this sense is a deepening understanding, a greater capacity to receive and to see anew the implications of revealed truth.

[31] Thomas P. Rausch, 'Development of Doctrine,' in *The New Dictionary of Theology*, eds. Joseph A. Komonchak, Mary Collins, and Dermot A. Lane (Wilmington, DE, 1987), p. 283.

In the latter part of the twentieth century, a number of scientific, technological and social factors impel those whose 'faith seeks understanding' to reflect with new urgency on the meaning of the lived body within Christian Revelation. As will be reiterated in the following chapters, it would not have been possible for a Theology of the Body to develop adequately prior to the present time. This is true partly because of the factors cited in this chapter, but also partly because of the interdisciplinary assistance now available for theological incorporation. The technological, audio-visual immediacy of people to one another is evoking theological reflection on body-centered issues as diverse as male-female relations, genetic experimentation, societal violence, and the fabrication of 'model' human beings.

For anyone participating in the development of a Theology of the Body, it is essential first to recognize the immense spectrum that the discipline spans. As Ratzinger notes, this extends from the 'wavicles' of matter tracked at dizzying speeds, to the inner perichoretic relations of trinitarian life. Second, theological reflection on the embodied person springs from what has been divinely revealed concerning the human vocation to be 'the image and likeness of God.' Third, within the development of doctrine concerning the revealed meaning of embodiment, the principle of *relationship* is paramount, particularly as exemplified in the Trinity, the Eucharist, and in the sacramental character of matter. Fourth, in Christian theologizing concerning the lived body, there must be an abiding awareness of the eschatological destiny of the whole body-person. Fifth, in approaching the study of body, the coinherence of Christian doctrines will prompt theologians to see the manner in which there is an illumination of body *meaning* from doctrine to doctrine. In this historical moment, such a relational approach allows a deepened understanding of the *nuptial* meaning of body. Francis Martin observes:

> If the body may properly be described as the revelation of the totality of the person and thus a sacrament, and if the body as sexually differentiated may be called nuptial, insofar as masculinity and femininity pertain to the interior uniqueness and originality of the person, it follows that sexuality is intrinsic or essential to the human person. This conclusion emerges from the

theology of the body of John Paul II.... It also, however, finds confirmation in recent proposals made by Walter Kasper and Karl Lehmann ... the ultimate referent of the nuptial character of the body, that to which it ultimately points, if only dimly and by analogy, is to the Trinitarian *communio*.[32]

Chapters Two through Four will place Theology of the Body within the larger framework of theological endeavor and begin to explore the body within the mystery of total personal identity. Chapters Five and Six consider the *vocation* to be embodied in the world, while Chapters Seven through Twelve study the implications of this vocation in the areas of sexuality, work, prayer, suffering, death and resurrection. What, then, is Theology of the Body?

---

[32] Francis Martin, *The Feminist Question*, p. 393.

2

What is Theology of the Body?

ALTHOUGH the term 'Body Theology' only came into promi-
nence in the 1960s, it is rooted in the core mysteries and
experience of the Judeo-Christian tradition. Scripture abounds
with graphic accounts of body-involvement in the giving and
receiving of Revelation. When Saul, en route to do violence to
Christ's followers, was personally encountered by the Risen
Lord, the meeting was not abstract or ethereal. It happened on a
well-traveled road, near a major city. He was struck forcibly in
his body, flung down to the ground. A Voice called him by
name, placing a question that would reverberate throughout his
entire life: 'Saul, Saul, why are you persecuting me?' (Acts 9:4).
The encounter with the Risen Christ involved his entire body-
person. When he asked, 'Who are you, Lord?' he received the
cryptic revelation that would shape his faith and mission: 'I am
Jesus, and you are persecuting me' (Acts 9:5). Temporarily
blinded from the encounter, Saul was led by the hand into
Damascus. There, without sight, neither eating nor drinking
for three days, he prayed and waited for the promise of the
Voice to be fulfilled: 'You will be told what you have to do'
(Acts 9:6).

Equally vivid in terms of body-involvement is the Genesis
description of the manner in which Abraham 'cut covenant' with
Yahweh. According to the covenantal custom of his time, Abraham cut in two the bodies of prescribed animals, placed them in
parallel rows, warded off desert vultures, and waited for the
covenantal presence of God, which was manifested as a perceptible fire-brand in the night. *In his body*, Abraham knew the
profundity of cutting covenant with God. Similarly, Moses was
surprised by the revealing presence in a burning bush when he
was tending sheep in the desert. Before receiving the revelation of
divine identity, he needed to approach the flaming bush, to
remove his shoes, and *bodily* know the desert environs as holy

ground. Much later, it was in the familiar context of mending fishing gear that Peter, James and John received the call to follow Jesus.

Body-involvement in the divine-human encounter is particularly replete in the account of Mary's visit to Elizabeth in the Judean hill country. According to Luke, the child in Mary's womb would have been in his first days or weeks of development when Elizabeth confirmed her cousin as 'Mother of my Lord.' Luke described the interpersonal meeting of four: when Mary's words of greeting evoked John's leap in her womb, Elizabeth cried out in grateful joy at the presence of the newly-incarnate Lord within Mary's body (see Luke 1:39–45). Later, after John's birth, his naming would occasion the release of Zechariah's tongue.

Christian faith is embodied faith, deriving from the incarnate Word, Jesus Christ, and the Revelation that he lived out bodily, but principally through his passion, death and resurrection. Christian theology (*fides quaerens intellectum*, faith seeking understanding) can be authentic only when it, too, is firmly rooted within the mystery of embodiment. Genuine faith understanding presumes a sound, ever-deepening anthropology: the significance of embodiment is crucial to all theological inquiry. Benedict Ashley observes: 'In fact any question I know how to ask concerns bodies, since even if something exists that is not bodily, I will know it only if somehow it contacts me as I am a body. Therefore, the puzzle of my body-self is a *universal* question, conditioning every other question I may ask.'[1] Ashley underscores the fact that Christian theology, of necessity, must grapple with the depth meaning of human embodiment.

BASIC QUESTIONS FOR A THEOLOGY OF THE BODY

This book, then, is intended as an introduction to Theology of the Body. It asks foundational questions that need to be probed in this particular theological discipline:

[1] Benedict Ashley, *Theologies of the Body*, p. 4.

How should the lived body be described?

What is the *meaning* of human embodiment?

What is the relationship of the human body to the rest of the material universe?

What does bodilyness contribute to an understanding of being made 'in the image and likeness of God'?

Why do Christians affirm that the ultimate divine Revelation has been given in and through the Incarnate Christ?

What is the significance of work?

Why are we sexual persons?

What does it mean to 'pray the body'?

What is the meaning of suffering, illness, aging and dying?

What is the destiny of the body-person after death?

While an introductory work cannot provide exhaustive discussion of these questions, they are reflected upon in a foundational manner and specific suggestions are made for ongoing theological study. From the outset, it is important to give a 'working definition' of the term 'Theology of the Body', and to discuss why it has taken on a specific identity at the threshold of Christianity's third millennium.

Theology of the Body can be described as *that discipline which reflects upon a faith understanding of the lived body and the material universe*. It utilizes what John Macquarrie has called the six factors formative of theology: experience, Revelation, Scripture, tradition, culture and reason.[2] While each factor is vital to an integral theology, there are tensions among them, and there are priorities to be respected in their interrelation. In a theological discipline that probes a faith understanding of the human body and the material universe, insights from related disciplines are not simply of casual interest: they assist in the deeper penetration of the mysteries of faith.

Why has it taken so long to recognize the need for a specific theological discipline devoted to a Theology of the Body? There

---

[2] See John Macquarrie, *Principles of Christian Theology*, 2nd ed. (New York, 1977), pp. 4–18.

are several reasons: 1) the human body can *seem* so familiar that commonly held descriptions and understandings have often been presumed sufficient for theological purposes (only when significant 'paradigm shifts' occur is there a new impetus for study and renewed probing);[3] 2) at this historical moment, new questions concerning the body have an immediacy which touches daily life, evoking the desire for swift, practical, theological response; and 3) in dealing with these issues, respect for individual choice has, for many, replaced a deeper theological search for the meaning, vocation and destiny of embodied persons. A brief discussion of each reason will help to explain why the explicit discipline, 'Theology of the Body,' emerged in the 1960s.

Familiar Understandings Can Seem Adequate

First, then, what it means to be an embodied human being can *seem* so familiar that there is no urgency for questioning it *theologically*. As Karl Rahner observed, being human is what we experience daily, 'what has been tried out and interpreted a billion times already in the history to which we belong, what each of us knows inside himself and outside himself in his environment.'[4] Yet, asked Rahner, do we really *understand* that? How doubtful, he said, that we really accept our humanity fully. 'Man is a mystery. Indeed he is *the* mystery.'[5] Only by walking ever more deeply into that mystery, he said, will we be able to ask what it really means to affirm that *the Word became flesh*. As has been seen in Chapter One, and as will be shown in ensuing chapters, the human body has been repeatedly misunderstood and denigrated during the course of Christian experience. What is held in contempt cannot be considered significant in the divine-human relationship. When embodiment is perceived as an obstacle to this relationship, there is a severe loss of theological and spiritual insight.

In the closing years of the twentieth century, there are varied

---

[3] See an outline comparative description of 'New-Paradigm Thinking in Science and Theology', in Fritjof Capra and David Steindl-Rast, *Belonging to the Universe: Explorations on the Frontiers of Science and Spirituality* (San Francisco, 1991), pp. xi–xv.

[4] Karl Rahner, 'On the Theology of the Incarnation,' in *Theological Investigations IV*, trans. Kevin Smyth (London, 1966), p. 107.

[5] Karl Rahner, 'On the Theology of the Incarnation,' p. 119.

attitudes toward the body among the diverse nations and cultures of the human community. To some, the lived body is unmanageable without the assistance of chemical and/or technological interventions; for others, the body is an object of individual ownership and incontestable personal decisions; for still others, who anguish over mass violence and degradation of body-persons, there is uncertainty concerning effective ways of remedying the situation. In addition, there are those who view the lived body as the supreme artifact, the material for deliberate re-fashioning. Spurred by the uncertainties of this century, those seeking a more profound faith understanding concerning embodiment have begun to press with new intensity the deeper questions evoked by Rahner's insight: what does it *mean* to be enfleshed, and what has the Incarnate Christ revealed in Person about 'becoming flesh'?

The Ever-Expanding Potential for Understanding Embodiment

There is a second and very practical reason for the vigorous development of body theology at the close of Christianity's second millennium: the dramatic advance and ready accessibility of knowledge concerning body/matter, attended by limitless potential for good and evil. The inner unity of the human person, matter and spirit, is so intimate and familiar that often it is only a crisis or the opening of totally new possibilities that will invite fresh concern about the lived body. There is an anomaly here: when the experience of pain, trauma, or severe limitation attends embodiment, there is a surge of desire to escape the predicament. In moments of crisis one has no time to ponder: what does this *mean*? When suffering is alleviated, we tend to distance ourselves from it rather than to probe its meaning.

In the twentieth century, bodily horrors have been inflicted on individuals, races and nations to an extent unimaginable in earlier periods of history. While some deny horrors such as the Holocaust during World War Two, others ask: how could this occur? what does it *mean*? how can this be prevented from occurring again? While there are divergent answers, the questions endure, and they further impel the development of a Theology of the Body.

The work of scientists and technicians provides valuable information to theologians. Matter itself has been entered and understood in new ways. A Theology of the Body would not have been able to emerge with the same scope and intensity prior to the twentieth century. Consider the insights received from the following: the splitting of the atom and a growing realization of the energy dynamically inherent in the material world; the discovery of DNA; the mapping of the human genome; the radical advances in surgery and medical treatments; and the globally-transmitted experience of treading on the surface of the moon. All of these have contributed to understanding 'the flesh' and matter, and they have raised new questions to be reflected upon in the light of Revelation, Scripture, and Tradition.

Bio-scientists have evoked new, intensely practical questions concerning sexuality, health, work, economic stability, illness and death. Since these questions affect bodily existence with such immediacy in a world community that is increasingly interconnected and exposed, there is a clamor for swift, practical resolution of dilemmas intimately associated with bodilyness. What previously would not have seemed to impinge directly upon personal and international life now cries out for speedy resolution (for example, responsibility for human fertility, and genetic manipulation).

Among Western nations, where Christian principles no longer provide a common unifying basis for personal and communal life, *individual choice* is considered an absolute to be safeguarded by law. Robert Brungs suggests, for example, that 'privacy' has become the great new constitutional idea in the United States. The nation is now

> ... comprised of two hundred and forty million little nations aggregated to each other by 'treaties.' This society is no longer held together by a communally accepted vision of reality. It is held together by a commonality of law, law which will become increasingly coercive as the fragmentation grows.... It is now more important than ever to understand what it means to be human – what our human potentialities are and what our human destiny is ...'[6]

The fragmentation of human choices and the loss of a common

[6] Robert Brungs, *You See Lights Breaking Upon Us* (St. Louis, MO, 1989), pp. 31, 37.

understanding concerning material reality spur theologians to address what it means to be human, to be expressed bodily, with a divinely-given vocation and destiny. In his 1979 Audiences, Pope John Paul II began laying foundations for a Theology of the Body, repeatedly emphasizing the urgency of the task.[7] As will be seen throughout this book, contemporary theologians and those who work in related disciplines hold differing presuppositions regarding Revelation, the fundamental meanings of truth, creation, the Incarnation, salvation, and resurrection. This results in differing scholarly responses to questions about the meaning and destiny of human life, such as: 1) are there enduring truths about the lived human body, or is humanity evolving in a manner that nullifies former doctrines? 2) is there an obligation to 're-create' human beings, eliminating what are perceived as undesirable traits, and equipping them for calculated projects? 3) how would a revised humanity relate to Jesus' Incarnation, to the meaning of sin and the need for redemption? and 4) what happened to the body of Jesus in the Paschal Event, and to the body of Mary in her Assumption, and what does this signify for the universal experience of suffering, death and eschatological fulfillment?

Human Invention or Divine Gift?

It is not difficult to see, then, why the present time evokes a Theology of the Body. The world community simultaneously knows immense threats and seemingly immeasurable promises of advance for embodied persons and the material universe. It is the former, however, that provide the basic grist for newscasts: civil wars accompanied by 'ethnic cleansing'; famine (often propelled by warring factions); AIDS and other sexually-transmitted diseases; government-funded abortions; and sophisticated weapons, which allow a few individuals to terrorize whole populations. The earth itself has been ravaged and poisoned, sometimes with the specific intent of destroying 'the enemy.' The flaming oil wells in the Persian Gulf War exemplified this abuse of earth.

[7] See Pope John Paul II, *Original Unity of Man and Woman*, Vatican trans. (Boston, MA, 1981); *Blessed Are the Pure of Heart: Catechesis on the Book of Genesis*, Vatican trans. (Boston, MA, 1983); *Reflections on Humanae Vitae*, Vatican trans. (Boston, MA, 1984); and *The Theology of Marriage and Celibacy*, Vatican trans. (Boston, MA, 1986).

More subtle is the ongoing commercial contamination of soil and environment.

Those who probe the meaning of faith in the enfleshment of the Second Person of the Trinity, and all that flows from his redemptive Self-gift and presence in creation must take seriously the questions that arise from new possibilities, since they have bearing on the central tenets of Christian faith. The present historical moment is a privileged time of opportunity and responsibility. Those who reflect upon body and matter theologically need to avoid both a sentimental sanguinity and an over-cautious fear concerning the volatile uses of technology which mark recent decades. Walter Kasper stresses that truth is foundational for linking theory and practice:

> What is truth? In everyday life the question about the truth is anything but theoretical. It is highly practical.... Only the truth helps us to behave in the way that reality enjoins, and lets us find our bearings in the conditions which make up our lives.... Once thinking has lost its reference to reality and its objectivity, what counts is no longer insight into the truth of anything. It is now only a matter of public acclaim, propaganda, publicity and entertainment.[8]

Since every human question concerns bodies in some way, it is vital to ask *what truth can be known about the body and its meaning*? As Kasper notes, in daily life, truth is anything but theoretical. 'Faith that seeks understanding' must be open to all truth so that there is the enablement of behaving 'in a way that reality enjoins.' Concern for truth underscores the importance of the questions posed for exploration in this theological discipline.

The human body participates in Rudolph Otto's familiar description of the holy. The holy, he said, is *mysterium tremendum fascinans*, a mystery simultaneously awe-inspiring and fascinating. The body is intimately involved in the mysteries of faith and holiness, the latter understood by Christians as an *embodied* holiness. The body can prove both fascinating and fearsome, leading some theologians to avoid or diminish foundational Christian beliefs concerning Christ's Incarnation.

[8] Walter Kasper, *Theology and Church*, trans. Margaret Kohl (New York, 1989), p. 134.

31

Walter Kasper notes that the mystery of the Word made flesh is the 'fundamental scandal' of the Christian faith. It can come as no surprise, he says, that the Council of Chalcedon's definition of this belief brings provocation today, even as it did in the early centuries of faith. After reflecting on the ways in which the dogma of the Incarnation is contested by some theologians today, Kasper writes that there is a difficulty still deeper than their contesting the mystery: 'The opposite would be closer to the truth. It is often no longer understood, and is pushed aside as being for people today an irrelevant and incomprehensible speculation.'[9]

The task of a Theology of the Body is to reflect on embodiment and the material universe in light of the perennial bases of Christian faith: the coming of God in the flesh in Jesus Christ and all that he accomplished, revealed and opened through his earthly life, death and resurrection as a totally new potential for every human being. Only from that basis can there be an authentic grappling with the theological significance of body in a time of radical transition, in a time when the very identity of what it means to be enfleshed is severely questioned. Among all theological disciplines, a Theology of the Body must be aware not only of Revelation, Scripture and Tradition, but also of the other crucial factors named by Macquarrie: culture, reason, and experience.

Further, theological reflection on body and matter must take into account the 'imagined future' and the impact of 'virtual reality.' Barbara Duden, for example, author of *The Woman Beneath the Skin*, thinks that the human body today is not what we commonly assume through discovery; rather, it is an 'invention,' in which the 'thinkable actually becomes reality.'[10] She holds that the body has changed significantly through history, prior to any contemporary technological interventions. Through studying the case notes of an early eighteenth-century German physician, Duden thinks that she has found traces of human embodiment that are different from the body we assume we know today. *Has* the body changed significantly already (or is it simply our *perceptions* that have changed, linked to our

---

[9] Walter Kasper, *Theology and Church*, p. 95.
[10] Barbara Duden, 'History Beneath the Skin,' CBC *IDEAS* Transcripts (Toronto, 1991), p. 6.

innovative genius)? In the following chapter it will be helpful to look briefly at key interdisciplinary insights that contribute to a deeper understanding of the lived body.

3

The Human Body: Mysterious and Relational

THE opening chapters of Genesis limn in bold strokes two complementary accounts of creation, each portraying the origins of the universe, the varieties of created beings, and the emergence of human life. There is a sophistication in these narratives, despite their brevity, their poetic but concrete narrative styles. Within a faith perspective, each attributes the origins of the universe and the coming-to-be of man and woman to a loving, personal Creator.

The older account, given in chapters two and three of Genesis, was probably written ca. 950 BC; it is sometimes termed 'Yahwist' since the author(s) speaks of the one God as 'Yahweh.' The text depicts a primordial intimacy between God and the original man and woman, and the impact that their sinful choices had on this relationship, extending from them to all of creation. The Yahwistic account is also termed 'anthropomorphic' since it describes God as fashioning humans 'by hand' and then interacting with them 'anthropomorphically,' that is, in ways characteristic of human beings.

The creation account in chapter one of Genesis, written or redacted perhaps in the sixth century BC, is referred to as the 'Priestly' account since its represents the focus of those responsible for maintaining faithful worship in the time of the Babylonian Exile. This narrative depicts the emergence of the known universe within a seven-day creative process. Here the divine Creator brings forth each kind of creature simply by divine intent and word, 'letting them be' as the narrative expresses it in liturgical poetic style. Despite their different approaches, both accounts affirm that creation culminates in the emergence of woman and man and reveal the specific human vocation to be in personal relationship with God and one another. Entrusted with responsibility for their fertility and for the care of all created things, the original man and woman are given to understand that there are limitations within their creatureliness: together with the call to respect these limitations, they experience the possibility of being deceived, of thinking that they are independently invincible, even equal to the God who brought them forth from non-being. The mysteries of creation, sketched so briefly in the opening chapters of the Hebrew Testament, will invite reflection until the end of time. Every truthful insight from the various sciences that examine life and the material universe contributes to the unfolding of the Genesis narratives and simultaneously assists the work of Theology of the Body.

For the purposes of this introductory book, we will consider just three major areas in which interdisciplinary findings/speculation contribute to theological insight regarding human embodiment and matter: 1) the mysterious qualities of matter; 2) the interrelationships within all of creation; and 3) the unpredictable aspects of matter and body.

MATTER AND BODY: PARTICIPANTS IN MYSTERY

Prior to the twentieth century there was little realization of the immense forces inherent in even minute forms of matter, whether these energies were in living bodies or layered in mammoth, rock-crusted mountains. What is enduringly puzzling for those devoted to academic and technological research is the 'something beyond' itself in matter that enables some creatures to move, breathe, and feel, and for human beings to experience thought, memory and love. Complete comprehension of the lived body always exceeds analytical insights obtained from empirical evidence.

The inextricable union of matter and spirit is the most basic mysterious quality of the lived body. How can it be that water drawn from springs below the earth's crust combines with carrots, lettuce and bread to form fingers or the arch of an eyebrow? More mysterious, how can vegetative and animal life assist the very *possibility of remembering* a Spanish coastline at sunrise, of *knowing* a complicated formula, or *professing love* through a marriage vow? How can this be? To know, remember, and love are primary human characteristics.

The lived body is not simply a material instrument, used to transmit what a 'real person' living within it thinks, remembers, and loves – it is not a robot that the 'real person' inhabiting it can replace with a more sophisticated model. Body and soul are not separate entities. A human person does not *possess* a body; rather, from the moment of conception, each is *expressed* bodily, so that no one can be distinguished from his/her body. As Jorg Splett points out, the identity of each person is established precisely on account of the body. Reflecting on this mysterious, integral unity he writes:

> The truth is that the fluid dialectical relationship of unity and opposition between body and soul can neither be transcended nor dissolved. And no completely satisfactory solution has been found for it in the whole history of thought.[1]

It has already been noted that 'any question I know how to ask concerns bodies.' It is now important to add: any question concerning the human body also concerns this mysterious union of matter and spirit. Add to this Karl Rahner's firm insistence that the understanding of what it *means* to be a human being is basic for receiving and understanding the meaning of the Incarnation, the divine Word become flesh.

Attempts to dismiss the reality of this unique union of matter and spirit recur throughout history. There are some who claim that the human person is *only* material and that all powers which have commonly been attributed to a 'soul' can be explained as biochemical processes inherent in living matter. This view is evidenced, for example, in the *Humanist Manifesto II* of 1973. Drawn up by a group of thinkers who wished to identify themselves as 'humanists,' the Manifesto expresses a world-view intended to serve as basis for shared action. In summarizing this document, Benedict Ashley shows how its proponents assume that the human species emerged from natural evolutionary sources. 'As far as we know,' they assert, 'the total personality is a function of the biological organism transacting in a social and cultural context. There is no credible evidence that life survives

[1] Jorg Splett, 'Body,' in *Sacramentum Mundi*, eds. Karl Rahner, Cornelius Ernst, and Kevin Smyth (Montreal, 1968), I, p. 234.

the death of the body.'[2] In this humanist perspective, there is no recognition of matter-spirit union. There are only 'biological organisms' that cease to exist after death.

In the 'developed' nations of the West, many perceive the living body instrumentally, either as a communications center, or a material residence for the person who inhabits it. Concomitant with such a perception of the lived body is the assertion that each individual 'owns' it as absolute, private property. Like other property that an individual possesses, the body can be utilized for a time, enhanced, sold for profit, partitioned, or disposed of when it loses market value. When the visible body becomes unsightly or proves to be a serious financial burden, its owner can dispose of it in a manner that seems of greatest benefit and least trouble. There are numerous variations of understanding the body in a strictly instrumental sense, but in each instance there is some denial of the indissoluble union that constitutes the human person.

Whether the human body is considered a completely material organism, or a mere instrument of a 'real person' who inhabits it, there is a by-passing of body-soul unity. Either assessment may seem to eliminate many problems and to enable an individual to resolve specific issues according to personal preference, but each involves a diminishment of *meaning*. If the human body is considered a mere material process, or an individual's private property, procreation and sexual activity lose their personal, relational significance; violent intrusions and technological manipulations become commonplace. The separable body is removed from the covenantal realm and is relegated to a legal, contractual status. For example, the conception of children under laboratory conditions or through surrogates, is hedged about by contracts which protect those who are parties to the arrangement. Increasingly, events surrounding health care and dying take place within a legal format. As will be seen in later chapters, an understanding of the indissoluble union of body and soul is foundational for the development of a Theology of the Body. The universal *Catechism of the Catholic Church* states that 'The human body shares in the dignity of "the image of God": it is a human body precisely because it is animated by a

---

[2] Benedict Ashley, *Theologies of the Body*, p. 55.

spiritual soul, and it is the whole human person that is intended to become, in the body of Christ, a temple of the Spirit.'[3] In #365, the *Catechism* asserts:

> The unity of soul and body is so profound that one has to consider the soul to be the 'form' of the body: i.e., it is because of its spiritual soul that the body made of matter becomes a living, human body; spirit and matter, in man, are not two natures united, but rather their union forms a single nature.[4]

In the *Instruction on Respect for Human Life in Its Origin and on the Dignity of Procreation*, issued by the Congregation for the Doctrine of the Faith in response to specific questions concerning procreation and biomedical interventions, it is stressed that the criteria for coming to decisions regarding these matters presuppose a proper understanding of 'the nature of the human person in his bodily dimension.'[5] The self-realization of the human person can be achieved only in terms of a unified totality that is both spiritual and corporeal:

> By virtue of its substantial union with a spiritual soul, the human body cannot be considered as a mere complex of tissues, organs and functions, nor can it be evaluated in the same way as the body of animals; rather it is a constitutive part of the person who manifests and expresses himself through it.[6]

Referring to an address by Pope John Paul II to members of the World Medical Association, the writers of the document stress that personal uniqueness is constituted by body as well as spirit: 'Thus, in the body and through the body, one touches the person himself in his concrete reality.'[7]

[3] *Catechism*, #364. In f.n. #232, the *Catechism* further refers to 1 Cor. 6:19–20; 15:44–45.
[4] In calling the soul the 'form' of the body, the *Catechism* cites the Council of Vienne (1312) as given in DS 902.
[5] See Congregation for the Doctrine of the Faith, *Instruction on Respect for Human Life in Its Origin and on the Dignity of Procreation: Replies to Certain Questions of the Day*, Vatican trans. (Boston, 1987), p. 8.
[6] Congregation for the Doctrine of the Faith, *Instruction on Respect for Human Life*, p. 8.
[7] Congregation for the Doctrine of the Faith, *Instruction on Respect for Human Life*, pp. 8–9. See also Pope John Paul II, 'Discourse to the Members of the 35th General Assembly of the World Medical Association,' October 29, 1983: *AAS* 76 (1984), p. 393.

BODY CENTERS THE PERSON IN THE UNIVERSE

The living body locates a person on earth, or on a space journey patterned from earth. The farther space-travelers move from earth, the greater the intensity of 'tracking' their location and presence, and of keeping the channels of communication open. Fictitious works portray the horror of 'being lost in space,' with no capacity to 'keep in touch' with other persons or 'get one's bearings.' Our bodies center us in the universe, making it possible for others to find us, not merely as objects or instruments, but as living, unique personal presences. These simple, even obvious observations underscore the reality that the human body exceeds mere empirical analysis.

The living and lived body is mysterious in the sense that Karl Rahner wrote of mystery. Mystery, he said, is not something that needs to be 'fetched.' Rather, it is the 'impenetrable which is already present.' It is not something to be overtaken, not something to be totally analyzed and factored when humanity attains an ultimate realization of its potential. Mystery, says Rahner, is the 'indomitable dominant horizon' that enables us to understand other things simply by the fact 'that it is silently there as the incomprehensible.'[8] It is within such a context of Mystery that the Genesis narratives introduce the meaning of the created universe and human existence, describing the emergence of sun and moon, plant, animal and human life in relation to the personal God who summons them all into existence.

The human capacity to enter mystery can be compared to the experience of entering an endless forest, where each turn in the path opens to the unforeseen. Although one can marvel over the immensity of redwood trees and the intricate needle-beds on the forest floor, it is impossible to grasp (even superficially) the content, forms of life, and subatomic activity within a square meter of the forest. Only by entering it with openness to its truths can one receive *something* of its inexhaustible reality and meaning, its interrelatedness with all that exists. The more that one comes to *know with the whole body-person* a single pine cone or

---

[8] Karl Rahner, 'On the Theology of the Incarnation,' p. 108.

a red squirrel pawing the forest floor, the more one will know the inexhaustible mystery of 'forest.' All this is said by way of metaphor. Mystery, said Rahner, is 'the propriety which always and necessarily characterizes God – and through him, us – so much so, that the immediate vision of God which is promised to us as our fulfilment, is the immediacy of the incomprehensible.'[9] Mystery is not something which will ultimately be surpassed: it is a gift to be received, but never totally grasped. Each advance into mystery invites a further entry, both revealing what was not previously understood, and pointing to a still vaster incomprehensibility.

Saul's experience on the road to Damascus exemplifies entrance into the immediacy of mystery. When he pursued Christians, he thought that he possessed a singular clarity regarding his mission, the nature of the problem to be solved, and the manner in which to achieve it. Actually, despite his dedication and practical methods, he only glimpsed the reality that so absorbed him. He knew that someone called Jesus had lived and had attracted a group of committed followers. From within his limited worldview Saul perceived them as a threat. In the *encounter* on the Damascus road, he was invited to enter the mystery that he had been treating as a problem to be solved. His experience of encounter with the living Risen Christ came dramatically in and through his body. Stunned and blinded, he literally groped his way into receptivity for the mystery of the Risen Christ and his presence within the Christian community.

Receiving rather than Grasping the Mystery of Embodiment

Studying and reflecting upon the living body-spirit as a received *mystery* removes the illusion that the lived body can be totally known by careful analysis. Theologically, it is a matter of receiving rather than grasping. The ever-increasing precision in scientific and technological research only confirms the need to approach embodiment as mystery. While it had been anticipated that refined instruments would eventually lead to total 'controllability,' researchers found that minute forms of matter become

[9] Karl Rahner, 'On the Theology of the Incarnation,' p. 108.

more elusive the more intimately they are studied. Scientific explanations for the origins of the universe often take on a mythic character. When COBE, the United States National Aeronautics and Space Administration's Cosmic Background Explorer satellite had seemingly discovered landmark evidence for the 'Big Bang' in 1992, astrophysicist George Smoot reported: 'If you're religious, it's like looking at God.'[10]

> According to the theory, the universe burst into being as a sub-microscopic, unimaginably dense knot of pure energy that flew outward in all directions, spewing radiation as it went, congealing into particles and then into atoms of gas. Over billions of years, the gas was compressed by gravity into galaxies, stars, planets and, eventually, even humans.[11]

In this brief description, the *language* is familiar, but it is impossible to fathom a 'dense knot of pure energy,' or 'billions of years.' Neither is it graspable that the size of the universe might have expanded 'by more than a trillion trillion trillion trillionfold in much less than a second,' nor that the swift rotation of the galaxies is held together by still undiscovered 'invisible halos of dark matter.'[12] This is poetic, mythical language, and in its own way is an acknowledgment of the mysterious quality of matter: the more that is known, the greater the opening into the unknown.

Only with advanced techniques has it become possible to perceive an aura surrounding the living body, although some persons had previously indicated their ability to detect such light patterns around the bodies of others. Initial research suggests that an 'aura' is a form of electromagnetic energy.[13] Likewise, only in recent decades has carbon-dating allowed the measurement of time. When mountain climbers discovered a naturally-mummified corpse in a melting Alpine glacier in September, 1990, radio-carbon testing determined that the man had lived approximately 4,600 years ago.

---

[10] See Michael D. Lemonick, 'Echoes of the Big Bang,' in *TIME*, 139, 18 (May 4, 1992), p. 62.
[11] Michael D. Lemonick, 'Echoes of the Big Bang,' p. 62.
[12] See Michael D. Lemonick, 'Echoes of the Big Bang,' p. 63.
[13] See Knight News Service, ' "Aura" Now Thought To Be a Type of Electro-magnetic Energy,' in *The Evening Sun*, Baltimore, MD (April 13, 1978), p. D1.

The ability to detect *something* of the origins of the universe –
a person's aura, or the age of a mummified corpse – is
significant: the more that is known of material reality only
opens to greater mystery. The ancients were awed by night
skies, noting the changed position of constellations even as they
assumed that the darkened dome above them appeared to be a
solid hemisphere studded with lights. Long before electrodes
and oscilloscopes were available, artists portrayed saints with
halos, signaling that a form of holy energy emanated from
them. Although much of the naivete concerning the nature of
stars and halos has dissipated, the mystery of matter can now be
entered with greater intensity.

While it is possible to date the approximate lifespan of the
oldest naturally preserved corpse, to photograph it and submit
it to various kinds of analysis, *the enduring meaning of embodiment* is a mystery freshly revealed through it. The meaning of
every human embodiment is questioned anew through the
mummified remains of the man who died in the icefields
millennia ago. What was his destination? Who awaited his
return? What is the enduring meaning of his body, not primarily
for those who study it and gaze upon it – but for the unnamed
man himself?

In asserting that truth is highly practical and that it helps us to
behave in a way that reality enjoins, Walter Kasper refers to the
insights of Thomas Aquinas. According to Thomas, says Kasper,
'truth is the self-manifestation of reality itself.'[14] This means that
the truths of persons and things are not determined by us individually: rather, by being open to the depths of their self-manifestation, we are able to act in accord with their reality – 'by cohering
with God's coherent order. Behind this understanding of reality
and truth is creaturely humility.'[15] Study of the body and the
material universe in this manner requires reverence and receptivity for the truths self-manifested in creation. Kasper distinguishes
between such an approach and the contemporary understanding
of *praxis*:

> For Thomas, everything real, inasmuch as it *is* real, is also true. In
> modern times this is no longer accepted. What is true is what

[14] Walter Kasper, *Theology and Church*, p. 135.
[15] Walter Kasper, *Theology and Church*, p. 136.

human beings have designed and made.... The human being no longer sees himself as part of the total cohesion and order of reality. Instead he makes himself reality's lord and creator. Human praxis no longer takes truth as its yardstick. Now truth is the expression and outcome of human praxis.[16]

Taking praxis as the basic criterion for what is true constitutes a serious obstacle not only for theologians, but for all who are committed to interdisciplinary search. Obversely, when there is appreciation for mystery and humility in encountering creation's self-manifestation, there can be a dynamic interaction among all academic and applied disciplines: the truths of reality become their common point of encounter.

Relationships Within Creation

Included in such an interdisciplinary approach to the living body and matter is the ever-expanding realization that all created reality is in relationship, consciously or unconsciously. There are innumerable forms of interdependence within the universe. Laboratory research, probes into outer space, and contemplative reflection on the data obtained through them have enhanced the human capacity to recognize the varieties of interdependence. At times, it is not contrived research but catastrophe that awakens insight and the recognition of truth. The truths of reality are frequently laid open violently through the wounds that humans inflict upon one another and upon the earth, evoking at least a superficial cumulative recognition of reality's truths and assisting us 'to behave in a way that reality enjoins.' In 1962, Rachel Carson's *Silent Spring* claimed that the central problem of this age is the contamination of the entire human environment. Plants, animals, and human cells which carry the heredity of past generations already bear accumulated contaminants capable of altering future generations. In *Pilgrim at Tinker Creek*, Annie Dillard relates that she watched sharks in a 'feeding frenzy' off the coast of Florida, noting the power, beauty and grace 'tangled in a rapture of violence.' She reflected:

[16] Walter Kasper, *Theology and Church*, p. 136.

43

We don't know what's going on here. If these tremendous events are random combinations of matter run amok, the yield of millions of monkeys at millions of typewriters, then what is it in us, hammered out of those same typewriters, that they ignite? We don't know. Our life is a faint tracing on the surface of mystery, like the idle, curved tunnels of leaf miners on the face of a leaf. We must somehow take a wider view, look at the whole landscape, really see it, and describe what's going on here.... After the one extravagant gesture of creation in the first place, the universe has continued to deal exclusively in extravagances, flinging intricacies ... on profligacies with ever-fresh vigor.[17]

As noted above, receptivity to Christ's Incarnation, the mystery of the Word made flesh, requires depth understanding of what it means to be expressed bodily as a human being. From its foundations, Christian theology presumes this, but it concomitantly requires awareness of the intricate interrelationships among all created beings.

Writing in the third century, when the human body was considered contemptible to many living in the Mediterranean basin, Tertullian gave Christian theology one of its foundational statements: *the flesh is the hinge of salvation*. He wrote in his *De resurrectione carnis*:

> To such a degree is the flesh the hinge of salvation, by which, with the soul, it is bound to God. It is the very flesh which makes it possible that the soul is able to be chosen by God. But also: the flesh is washed in order that the soul may be cleansed; the flesh is anointed in order that the soul may be consecrated; the flesh is signed in order that the soul may be fortified; the flesh is overshadowed by the imposition of the hand in order that the soul may be illumined by the Spirit. The body feeds on the flesh and blood of Christ so that the soul might feast upon God. Therefore, those things which work joins together are not able to be separated in reward.[18]

The lived body is simultaneously the turning point or hinge for divine-human relationships and the relationship of humanity

---

[17] Annie Dillard, *Pilgrim at Tinker Creek* (New York, 1974), pp. 8–9.
[18] Tertullian, *De resurrectione carnis*, ed. Ernst Evans (London, 1960), 8:6–12. Cited portion trans. by Sister M. Timothy Prokes.

with the rest of the material universe. The writer of Psalm 8, marveling at the spectacular works of creation prayed: 'Ah, what is man that you should spare a thought for him, the son of man that you should care for him?' (Ps. 8:4). To ancients, who wrote from a world-view that considered earth a stable mass, set on firm foundations, and who did not have the advantage of tools that probe atoms and body cells, there was no realization that human flesh was in a constant interchange of elements common to sand, fish and palm fronds. The human body is actually a living crossroad, a midway point between the most distant galaxies and the most minute subatomic particles. Some elements now present in our bodies derive from distant parts of the universe. Through the air we breathe, the food we ingest – even through our most casual contacts with other creatures, we are giving and receiving elements common to meteors, cougars and kelp. Physicists and biochemists confirm that elements within the human body can factually be termed *stargifts*. In his text *Biology*, Aaron Wasserman wrote that there was a statistical probability that an electron from a page of his book may *now* be at the far reaches of the Milky Way.[19]

There are infinitesimal distances *within* atoms where dynamic transactions occur at speeds beyond human comprehension. Other exchanges cross vast spatial distances. From the outset of theological reflection on the lived body a foundational principle to be confirmed is this: the created universe is a realm of constant interchange, of giving and receiving. Not only do human body-persons *participate* in this cosmic sharing: they enflesh the vocation of responsible stewardship, the call to incorporate all of creation into conscious praise of the triune Creator. Quantum theory, says Timothy McCarthy, has, in effect, turned 'material existence as we had long conceived of it into a metaphor: Nothing exists in itself, but only as an interconnection with something else – and that something else as an interconnection with something else – and so on to the reaches of the universe.'[20]

Physicists use the metaphorical language of 'waves and particles' to describe the dynamism of atomic elements. When scrutinized by researchers, the smallest elements of matter can

[19] See Aaron O. Wasserman, *Biology* (New York, 1973), p. 20.
[20] Timothy McCarthy, 'Reality as Cosmic Dance,' in *National Catholic Reporter*, December 11, 1987, p. 8.

appear to resemble either particles or waves, but never simultaneously. Further, those desiring to 'observe' them cannot measure their velocity and position at the same time. The minute forms of created matter elude human graspability. The very act of measuring them, and the instruments utilized, change their dynamic activity and appearance. Researchers have learned that *they themselves are part of the reality being studied.* 'What Heisenberg discovered that changed, perhaps forever, our perception of reality, is that, at bottom, we cannot observe a physical process without somehow affecting it, because we are part of the process.'[21] The physicist who glimpses the action of subatomic particles is simultaneously studying the truth of his/her own vibrant body.

In the time that it takes to read the previous sentence, an immense change has already occurred in the body-person of the reader. As Dossey notes, human genes are constantly renewed with protein units in a stream of shuffling and replacing. As a result of his work with radioisotope tracings, Paul Aebersold is convinced that ninety-eight per cent of all atoms in the average individual are replaced annually; thus, it can be presumed that the entire body is renewed to the last atom in about five years. What seems to be 'this too, too solid flesh' is a flow of existence. 'A strictly bounded body does not exist.'[22] While the subatomic interflow of all being, living and non-living, does not *define* reality, it points to the mystery of unitive meaning in material creation. Cogent observations attributed to two physicists speak into the work of Theology of the Body: Niels Bohr saying 'When it comes to atoms, language can be used only as poetry,' and Fritjof Capra conjecturing that perhaps half of United States physicists are in their particular scientific discipline because of the mysticism involved.[23]

BODY AND PERSONAL IDENTITY

How can the identity of the human person endure and deepen despite the constant interchange just described? The totality of

[21] Timothy McCarthy, 'Reality as Cosmic Dance,' p. 8.
[22] Larry Dossey, *Space, Time and Medicine* (Boulder, CO, 1982), p. 75.
[23] See Timothy McCarthy, 'Reality as Cosmic Dance,' p. 8.

interrelationships that mingle *within* a person both integrate and exceed what has been said of material exchange. Yet, personal identity endures. Benedict Ashley compares the individual person to a river; unlike a flowing stream, however, which dissipates traces of identity, the changing body retains the accumulating past and there is continuity in each person's unique personal history.

When DNA (deoxyribonucleic acid), the two-stranded fundamental molecule of life which bears the genetic code of an individual, was discovered in the 1950s, another avenue was opened for understanding human interrelationships. The genetic code contains the chromosomes of the original fertilized cell that initiates all further human development. The strands of forty-six human chromosomes are paired, twenty-three each received from male and female in the conception of a child. Each strand bears a distinct history, so that every newly-conceived human life bears a unique combination of possibilities and liabilities flowing from past generations. While this can be understood in new ways since the discovery of DNA, the history of salvation shows the significance of genealogies. The Gospels according to Matthew (1:1–17) and Luke (3:23–38), while differing in specific names and purpose, give detailed lists of Jesus' ancestry. Robert Brungs points to the incredibly narrow window of possibility that a *given* person exists: 'We know now that, if *I* had been conceived one maternal cycle earlier or one cycle later, I would not be *I*.'[24] Someone else, some other expression of the historical lineage would have been conceived, bearing another identity. Every person uniquely bears the wounds and gifts of those who have contributed to their genetic code.

In the mid-twentieth century, when Watson and Crick published their findings concerning the DNA molecule, there was also much theological dialogue concerning the possibility that the human family could have stemmed from a single original pair. The theory of *polygenism* was favored by many, who suggested that *homo sapiens* emerged through a number of ancestors when evolutionary development proved favorable. Subsequent research, however, indicated a different theory. In the 1970s it was found that *mitochondrial* DNA from outside a

[24] Robert Brungs, *You See Lights Breaking Upon Us*, p. 172.

cell's nucleus contains information helpful in tracing genealogies since it reveals only the genetic inheritance which has been received from the mother. Ensuing research in the 1980s proved astounding and provocative. A group of anthropologists, trained also in molecular biology, studied an international assortment of genes derived from mitochondrial DNA and perceived a genetic trail that led to a single mother from whom every human being has descended. Whether one called her 'Eve' or simply the common ancestral mother of the human family, the researchers spoke of humanity's common origin in a manner resonating with the theological narrative of Genesis. The 'original mother' of humanity, researchers estimated, would have lived perhaps 150,000 to 200,000 years ago. Geneticist Dr. Jerome Lejeune of the University of Paris said that it was not possible to describe her appearance or to indicate her location on earth. To do so is mere conjecture.[25] Mitochondrial DNA gives no indication of racial distinctions and it shows few genetic differences among cultures.

Guy Murchie, after consulting geneticists (including J. B. S. Haldane, Theodosius Dobzhansky and Sir Julian Huxley) asserted that relationships among all members of the human family are surprisingly close. No member of the human family, whatever their race, 'can be less closely related to any other human than approximately fiftieth cousin.'[26] Family genealogies meet and merge into one genetic family 'tree' by the time they have extended fifty generations. A father's and mother's family trees will inevitably overlap:

And as cells metabolize and circulate in the body, so do bodies and their genes circulate throughout mankind, joining everyone to everyone at least once in fifty generations, so that not only does the ancestry of each of us include all fertile humanity of fifty generations ago, but our descendants fifty years hence in turn will include every living being.[27]

[25] See Jerome Lejeune, 'Origins of Man,' McGivney Lectures, St. Catherine's Auditorium, Providence Hospital, Washington, D.C., October 26, 1993. (McGivney Lecture Series available on audio-tape from John Paul II Institute for Studies on Marriage and Family, Washington, D.C.)
[26] Guy Murchie, *The Seven Mysteries of Life* (Boston, MA, 1978), p. 345.
[27] Guy Murchie, *The Seven Mysteries of Life*, p. 357.

Such research interests theologians not because it verifies the Scriptures (which are not scientific writings). It is of theological assistance to the extent that it makes known something of reality's self-manifestation, something of the truths inherent in creation, *as halting, incomplete, and open to revision as such research may be at any given moment.* It extends the natural horizons and invites deeper entry into the mysteries of faith.

When Saul was bodily thrust to the earth and experienced the Risen Lord asking, 'Why are you persecuting *Me*?' he had to explore the meaning of universal relationship. For the rest of his life he would have to grapple with the implications of that experience, knowing that every follower of Christ that he had intended to arrest was already in some manner in union with Christ and with him, Saul. He was *physically plunged into the fundamental question of his life,* the mystery of embodied interrelatedness in Christ.

4

The Body: Both Familiar and Unknown

THE previous chapter introduced ways in which scientific and technological disciplines contribute to a theological understanding of the lived body and the material universe, particularly in regard to 1) mystery and 2) interrelatedness. There is a third major way in which a Theology of Body is enriched by interdisciplinary insights: those which illumine what might be termed the 'coincidence of familiarity and strangeness' in the human experience of embodiment. Philosopher Richard Zaner writes:

> I venture to suggest that Freud's ways of grappling with what he calls the uncanny (*Unheimliche*) provide a suggestive framework for understanding the sense of the body's otherness. There are four moments: a sense of helplessness and inescapableness, of dread and chilling fear, of hiddenness or concealment, and of the radically strange yet familiar (*Heimliche*). To understand my being embodied, I suggest, requires understanding the senses in which my own-body is experienced by me as 'uncanny.'[1]

The first of four 'uncanny' qualities of embodiment, then, is *inescapability*. Regardless of personal preference, each human being is expressed bodily with a particular bio-neurological-anatomical makeup. This simultaneously involves radical limitations. The desire to elude limitation leads some to resort to cosmetic surgery or to the use of chemical/technical means of altering what seems inadequate to them. Nevertheless, as Zaner points out, we are 'irrevocably determined in our lives by intrinsic limitations of organic embodiments in whose selection none of us had the least initial choice.'[2] We must come to terms

[1] Richard Zaner, *The Context of Self: A Phenomenological Inquiry Using Medicine as a Clue*, (Athens, OH, 1981), p. 50.
[2] Richard Zaner, *The Context of Self*, p. 51.

50

with them even when technological interventions allow the exchange of one set of limitations for another. Added to the received genetic inheritance of any given person are inner attitudes, and habits which, reinforced through repetition, impact the entire body-person. Since the body is 'lived,' it is inescapable that established patterns of behavior influence facial contours, gestures, and the subtle processes of organic systems. The first uncanny quality of embodiment, then, is 'inescapability' which involves multiple forms of limitation.

This is closely linked to a second uncanny quality: the experience of the total person being *implicated* in the body's conditions and functions. At times it can seem that 'the body' has failed us, as if it were 'over against us' rather than being our very identity outwardly manifest. The realization of being totally implicated in every aspect of our embodiment becomes especially acute when we are prevented from fulfilling basic needs or our compelling desires. The ability to think, remember and will can be severely impeded by bodily injury or the ordinary processes associated with aging. In turn, because of body-soul union, unresolved disturbances of an intellectual or emotional nature can result in severe physical trauma. While the term 'psychosomatic' has become a household word, the truth expressed by it is not commonly understood in its multiple ramifications.[3] The I-body is a unity: I am totally implicated in whatever is experienced, whether I advert to it or not.

Zaner observes that finding oneself implicated in whatever happens to the embodying organism, can be described as a

---

[3] An obvious example of this is the manner in which abortion and the search for ever more simplified means of procuring or inducing an abortion are discussed in the media. In a television interview with CNN (August 31, 1995) gynecologist Dr. Richard U. Hausknecht, proposing the inducement of abortions through the combined use of methotrexate (a drug used in cancer treatment) and misoprostol (a medication for ulcers) dismissed the impact that an early abortion would have upon a woman who experienced it in the privacy of her own home. He said that a woman who determined that she had an 'unwanted pregnancy' after missing a menstrual period would eliminate something no larger than a button, something unrecognizable as a fetus. *The Washington Post* (August 31, 1995, p. A5) reported that since scant studies support the use of this method of abortion, and since doctors are vulnerable to malpractice suits, Dr. Hausknecht urges women to use it as part of a 'controlled clinical trial' and asserts that a half-hour counseling session is essential since 'The bleeding and cramping can be unpleasant.... They could panic if they don't know what to expect. I explain it in graphic terms.'

'chill' of implicatedness. The entire body-person is irrevocably involved in whatever the body suffers, but is also susceptible to whatever might happen to material things generally.[4]

CRISES AND THE 'CHILL OF IMPLICATEDNESS'

In the aftermath of a serious accident that severs a limb or threatens life itself, there is a ruefulness concerning what 'might have been.' Veterans who participated in events marking the fiftieth anniversary of the conclusion of World War Two confirmed the depth implications of all body-experiences. Survivors of the invasion at Normandy wept as they related vivid memories: the crumpled bodies of comrades; coastal waters reddened with blood, and the morning sky laced with tracer bullets. Fifty years later, their lived bodies retained the events as if they had just occurred.

While Zaner deals mainly with the 'chill' of implicatedness, the positive aspect of total personal implication in whatever affects the body is also extremely important as a theological referent. It will be seen in later chapters how crucial this becomes in regard to understanding the Incarnation, Eucharist, and the Paschal Mystery in relation to the human vocation to be image of the triune God. The 'chill' of implication that comes with singular acuteness in times of crisis can be extremely positive. In her book *Seven Years Solitary*, Edith Bone described the manner in which she not only survived extended solitary confinement in a mid-twentieth century Budapest prison, but also became a more integrated human being. She knew that her captors were determined to 'break' her through darkness and isolation, but she resolved to survive and to utilize physical confinement as an *opportunity*. Approximating the length of her cramped cell, she estimated how many times she would have to cross it in order to cover the distance needed to reach various European destinations that she had formerly visited. She imag-

---

[4] See Richard Zaner, *The Context of Self*, p. 52.

ined the sights, sounds and smells that would be encountered at specific points in her journeys. Building upon her lifelong desire to learn advanced mathematics, she constructed a crude abacus from beads of hardened brown bread and straws plucked from a cleaning broom. She first used it to keep a numerical record of the vocabulary words she could recall from seven languages. When guards placed a weak light in her cell, she persuaded one to bring mathematics texts so that she might teach herself. Liberated after seven years, Edith was more accomplished, more integrated as a whole person than she had been prior to incarceration.[5]

Both Hebrew and New Testaments are permeated with accounts of the 'chill of implicatedness' and the ways in which it was either received as gift or rejected. In the story of Joseph, the favored youth's brothers lowered him into a well and drew him up only to sell him into slavery. Later, when his family was threatened by starvation, he was significant in assuring their sustenance. Joseph was a forerunner of Moses, whose vulnerable infant body was protected in a basket hidden among bulrushes. Throughout Scripture, Revelation is closely associated with body-centered experiential knowledge. It also gives evidence of the desire to escape the implications of embodiment. King Saul fell upon his sword and Judas hanged himself, each attempting to escape the condition of being outwardly manifest in the world.

In Gethsemane, according to the passion account of Luke, Jesus was so aware of being implicated in the body that he prayed more earnestly in his anguish 'and his sweat fell to the ground like great drops of blood' (Lk. 22:44). The early Christian hymn incorporated in Philippians (2: 6–11) celebrates Christ's 'emptying himself' into the human condition, becoming as humans are in all things but sin. To assume the human condition means vulnerability in and through the body. In the twentieth century, the potential to invade and/or torture the body-person or utilize the body for commercial purposes has surpassed any previous moment of history. Increasingly, there is the technical capability to change future generations irrevocably.

---

[5] See Edith Bone, *Seven Years Solitary* (London, 1957).

The Interior Body: A Hidden Presence

Zaner cites a third uncanny quality of embodiment, what he terms a 'hidden presence.' He refers to structured events and interchanges within the body which proceed without being consciously willed or, for the most part, observed: food is digested; the heart beats rhythmically; oxygen is drawn into the lungs and distributed with incredible finesse. Far more subtle, but, again (unless deliberately altered) apart from deliberate choice, are glandular secretions which significantly affect a wide range of total-body-person processes – either promoting a sense of well-being or disrupting a myriad of delicate balances within the whole person. It is possible to live for indefinite periods of time without adverting to these intricate interior phenomena, yet they are the hidden processes that allow innumerable *conscious* activities. Abuse of the body evokes disruptions among processes which ordinarily are outside the realm of conscious concern. There is an abiding need to respect the inner tempo.[6] Defying what Zaner terms the interior 'hidden presence' has implications that exceed matters of health and touch upon the understanding of sacramental life, particularly eucharistic dimensions of body given and received. Traumatic experiences, whether they originate predominantly in the 'I-body' or in the spiritual dimensions of intellection, volition or memory, affect those processes that ordinarily are outside the realm of our advertence. They can also awaken specific awareness of what has previously remained hidden.

In recent decades there has been a revived interest in those mystics who, through supernatural assistance (according to the evidence presented by contemporaries), may have transcended ordinary means of maintaining hidden body processes. While it is beyond the scope of this introductory study to expand on these extraordinary manifestations in detail, it is important to note that mystically-related phenomena such as sustenance without ordinary food and drink, ecstasies, visions, locutions, and levita-

---

[6] 'My embodying organism is thus always a *hidden-presence*, a latency thanks to which anything else can be or become patent. These hidden 'goings-on,' finally, are biologically rhythmed and conditioned with respect to my awarenesses even of my own body – such that I often find it necessary to adjust my own wishes, plans, desires to their tempo.' Richard Zaner, *The Concept of Self*, p. 54.

tions have been part of the Christian mystical tradition. These phenomena have significance for theological reflection because 1) they underscore the still largely unknown possibilities of graced embodiment; and 2) they are often linked to the Eucharist and thus invite further entrance into the mystery of body-given.[7] Diane Ackerman writes:

> Mysticism transcends the here and now for loftier truths unexplainable in the strait-jacket of language; but such transcendence registers on the senses, too, as a rush of fire in the veins, a quivering in the chest, a quiet, fossil-like surrender in the bones. Out-of-body experiences aim to shed the senses, but they cannot. One may see from a new perspective, but it's still an experience of vision.[8]

There is a fourth uncanny quality of embodiment which Zaner terms 'alien presence': 'My body is at once familiar and strange, intimate and alien: *"mine" most of all yet "other" most of all*, the ground for both subjective inwardness and objective outwardness ... the ground for both intimacy and distance, the near and the remote ... ultimately as the locus of that most alien of all: my own death.'[9] The body through which plans, goals and wishes are realized at times *seems* in some ways to have a life of its own.

Being awakened to the alien-like quality of one's body happens in different ways. It may come through the simple experience of seeing a friend or relative after a decade's absence and observing how they have aged: the other's appearance serves as a mirror of the self, encapsulating in a moment the changes accumulated

---

[7] As an introduction to this recent field of study, e.g. see Rudolph M. Bell, *Holy Anorexia* (London, 1985); and Elizabeth Alvilda Petroff, ed. *Medieval Women's Visionary Literature* (Oxford, 1986). There is a tendency today to utilize the techniques of contemporary analysis in evaluating the authenticity of those who claimed to be sustained physically only by the reception of the Eucharist. Our purposes obviate any attempt to suggest conclusions in this regard, but, rather, they are cited within the context of showing the immense realm opened by Theology of the Body.

[8] Diane Ackerman, *A Natural History of the Senses* (New York. 1991), p. 301, cited by J. Ruffing in 'You Fill Up My Senses: God and Our Senses,' *The Way* (April, 1995), p. 103. See Ruffing, pp. 103–104 for distinctions between 'sensuousness' and 'sensuality,' with particular reference to Charles Davis' *Body as Spirit: The Nature of Religious Feeling* (New York, 1976), pp. 42–43.

[9] Richard Zaner, *The Concept of Self*, p. 54.

slowly over the course of a decade. For others it may come through the amputation of a limb,[10] a stroke, or the impairment of vision.

It is relatively easy to identify experiences which correspond to Zaner's four modes of the 'uncanny' body. Already, however, there are other disconcerting possibilities which will inevitably increase a sense of the *Unheimliche*. Among these disconcerting possibilities are the patenting of life forms, burgeoning forms of bioengineering, and multiple forms of controlling the beginning and the end of human life. Robert Brungs asks, 'What if our deliberate use of microbiological techniques to "foster our evolution" is something God wants? What if the deliberate changing of our bodies is somehow needed in the development of the Kingdom of God? It's not a question, I think, that we can *automatically* dismiss.'[11] Brungs opines that theologically and ecclesially, there has been a loss of several decades in pursuing the enormous task of understanding what it means to be human. Beyond all of the phenomena, whether of a pedestrian, or scientific/technical, or mystical nature, there is the question of meaning and purpose. *Why* are human beings expressed bodily? From where does this meaning derive and how can it be recognized? Dermot Lane, pointing to the inadequacies in modern anthropology, holds for a need to construct an alternate way of 'looking at what it means to be human.' In light of calls to 're-invent the human,' to 'replace a narrow anthropocentric sensibility,' to rethink what it means to be a self, and construct what is termed a 'chastened anthropocentricity,' there is need to ask 'what is involved in being a person fully alive.'[12] Having surveyed some of the predominant interdisciplinary issues concerning embodiment, we now ask: within faith seeking understanding, what does it *mean* to be expressed in a body?

[10] See Charles Wagner, 'Body Totality: The Experience of Phantom Limb Pain. Theological and Pastoral Reflections,' Thesis, Newman Theological College, Edmonton, Alberta, 1992, (microfilm: National Library of Canada). Wagner's work deals particularly with the spiritual anxiety suffered by amputees.
[11] Robert Brungs, 'Hybrids, Genes and Patents,' in Institute for Theological Encounter with Science and Technology *Bulletin* (St. Louis, MO, Summer, 1995), p. 15.
[12] See Dermot A. Lane, 'Anthropology and Eschatology,' *Irish Theological Quarterly*, 61, 1 (1995), p. 14.

5

Embodiment as Vocation

CHRISTIAN faith affirms that the *meaning* of the lived body derives from the Creator. As the two accounts of creation in the opening chapters of Genesis reveal, body-meaning is given within the human vocation to be the image and likeness of God. It is not determined by individual choice, nor has it developed by chance as an aspect of evolution. Yet there is often great difficulty in interpreting body-meaning from a faith perspective. Chapter One surveyed some predominant ways in which the body has been misunderstood: at times rejected and despised, at times over-glorified. Faith understanding does not exist in isolation, so that the cultural, philosophical and political forces characteristic of any given historical period condition the manner in which Revelation and Tradition are theologically received and interpreted. In the present age, so assiduous in amassing factual data, and astute in the practice of analysis and innovation, there is a tendency to treat body-persons segmentally and to reconstruct the body and its meaning imaginatively without reference to the intent of the Creator.

If human life in the material universe bears an inherent vocation that refers to the entire body-person, that vocation emanates from a source that transcends humanity itself. No authentic 'call' can be self-induced, or elicited by talking-to-oneself, either individually or communally. A vocation is a gift: it can be recognized and then received (or misunderstood and/or rejected). Within Christian faith in divine Revelation, the gift of embodiment derives from God who, from love, created humanity, male and female, and revealed their basic human vocation. Body-meaning, then, is to be found primarily 1) in the original creation of human beings (precisely where Pope John Paul II began laying the foundations for his Theology of Body in the 1979 Audiences); 2) in the perfect fulfillment of body-meaning in Jesus Christ; and 3) in the illumination these provide regarding the meaning of every human body: its sacramentality, its temporal and eschatological significance. There is a seamless unity among these sources, and the ensuing chapters will discuss them in an introductory manner as an entry point into Theology of the Body.

First, then, consideration of body-meaning begins with human origins. In the creation narratives of Genesis, creation takes place in the context of dialogue, of personal divine word and act, and loving purpose. Cipriano Vagaggini writes:

> In the imaginative account of the creation of man in Genesis, God with greatest care forms the body and then the soul with his breath (Genesis 2:7–22). The whole concrete man, body and soul, was made in God's image insofar as the whole man is called to exercise his dominion over all creation as a stewardship (Genesis 1:26–28).... The fall is the fall of concrete man, both body and soul, and 'death' which is its punishment in the Bible is both a physical and a spiritual death, one implying the other.... In the creation and the fall as well as in the redemption, the body is no less subject and object than the soul.[1]

Robert Dickinson discusses the way in which both Old and New Testaments reflect the same concept of 'body' as 'an integral part of human personality, morality and destiny.'[2] In the Old Testament, words used to indicate the body or specific parts of the body (such as those employed for belly, flesh, back, bone, soul, substance and flesh) all refer to the physical entity, says Dickinson: 'No distinction is made in these terms between the physical and spiritual nature of mankind.'[3]

When the writers of the Hebrew Testament desired to emphasize physical aspects of the *whole* living human being, they employed the word *basar*; when they emphasized spiritual aspects of the living human being, they used *nephesh*. In the New Testament, the Greek word *sarx* signified the flesh in its weakness, its earthiness and corruptibility, but it was understood to be inseparable from the entire person. The Greek term *soma* had a more encompassing meaning and referred to the whole person as

[1] Cipriano Vagaggini, *The Flesh Instrument of Salvation: A Theology of the Human Body* (Staten Island, NY, 1969), pp. 20, 21.
[2] Robert Dickinson, 'Faith-Healing and Death,' *Irish Biblical Studies*, 15 (June, 1993), p. 129.
[3] Robert Dickinson, 'Faith-Healing and Death,' p. 129.

a physical entity. John A. T. Robinson says of the writings of St. Paul that it is no exaggeration to say that the concept of body is the keystone of his theology and that the word *soma* 'knits together' Paul's great themes:

> It is from the body of sin and death that we are delivered; it is through the body of Christ on the Cross that we are saved; it is into His body the Church that we are incorporated; it is by His body in the Eucharist that this Community is sustained; it is in our body that its new life has to be manifested; it is to a resurrection of this body to the likeness of His glorious body that we are destined. Here, with the exception of the doctrine of God, are represented all the main tenets of the Christian faith – the doctrines of Man, Sin, the Incarnation and Atonement, the Church, the Sacraments, Sanctification, and Eschatology.[4]

The Scriptures, whether Old or New Testaments, assumed that the human being was a unity of matter and spirit. There were no Hebrew equivalents for 'body' and 'soul' since it was understood that only the living, embodied male or female existed. Thus, Hebrew creation accounts differ emphatically from creation stories of other ancient civilizations. The Babylonian myth, *Enuma elish*, for example, portrayed the male god Apsu and his consort Tiamat begetting other gods, with earthly creatures coming into existence through violence: Apsu was slain by his offspring Ea, while Tiamat was killed by Ea's son. Marduk then fashioned the world from Tiamat's remains and *humanity was formed from the blood of Tiamat's slain counselor.* For the Canaanite neighbors of the Israelites, earthly 'beginnings' emerged from already existent matter through the instrumentality of the god El and his consort Asherah. According to the Egyptian theology of Heliopolis, human beings originated from the semen of the god Re. In these ancient myths, creation was perceived to be a result of sexual encounter or violence among gods and goddesses. There was a presumption that some primordial materials were utilized (as chaotic as these might have been). The creation of human beings was perceived to be a punishment or a diminished form of existence.

The Israelites, on the other hand, recorded their reflections on

[4] John A. T. Robinson, *The Body* (London, 1952), p. 9.

'the beginnings' *after* experiencing a covenantal relationship with a personal, loving Creator. The Priestly account in Genesis 1 reflects a communal experience of God. Firmly tethered to that experience, the writer(s) groped a way back though Abraham and covenantal faith to the origins of creation. In asserting that God created the world 'by his word,' says Michael Schmaus, the text expresses 'the fact that dialogue constitutes the basis of the relationship between God and the world. God did not create the world simply to have it on hand, but because he wanted to enter into communication and conversation with it. This has meaning only if we see man as the essential element in creation.'[5]

The identity and meaning of human life is directly related to divine life. John Courtney Murray, commenting on the revelation of the divine Name to Moses, notes that the chosen liberator of the Israelites was not making a calm inquiry about the inherent attributes of God: he was anxiously searching to know God's attitude toward himself and the whole people. For the Hebrews, a name defined the person (and thus to be 'no name' meant worthlessness). When asking the identity of the One who addressed him from the flaming bush, Moses pressed to know the Name: *who* shall I say sent me? While there are several possible interpretations of the compact Hebrew term used to express the divine revelation (a form of the ancient Hebraic verb 'to be') Murray said that to retain its full suggestion and maintain the paranomastic cadence of the original, one might translate the revealed divine Name in this manner: 'I shall be there as who I am shall I be there.'[6] There is a threefold significance in the revealed name. First, the revealing God is faithfully present in the history of the people (I shall be there). Second, the mystery of God's being is expressed, transcending any inner *necessity* in relation to creation (I shall be there as who I am). Third, despite the transcendence of divine inner mystery, 'God becomes transparent to his people.'[7] (I shall be there as who I am shall I be there.)

Such intimacy between the Creator God and humanity was already affirmed within the material setting of the Genesis

---

[5] Michael Schmaus, *Dogma 2: God and Creation* (New York, 1969), p. 71.
[6] John Courtney Murray, *The Problem of God, Yesterday and Today* (New Haven, CT, 1964), p. 10.
[7] John C. Murray, *The Problem of God*, p. 15.

accounts. The tree of life at the center of Eden represented a touchstone for covenantal fidelity. Between Creator and the first humans there was a shameless, uncloaked transparency of intimacy. The Yahwist narrates that the choice 'to be as God' involved whole body-persons; it disrupted the internal unity of matter and spirit, set male and female in opposition, and infected relationships between humanity and the whole of creation. The results of sin extended into the material universe, wounding all relationships. The Scriptures clearly express a belief that the Creator did not abandon woman and man after their separative choice. Genesis, written after repeated accounts of sinful falling away from covenant, assures belief that *the human vocation to be image and likeness of God endures despite the divisive wounding of sin* (see the proto-evangelium, Gen. 3:15).

The creation accounts of Genesis were focal for the series of Audiences which Pope John Paul II initiated on September 5, 1979, in which he reflected on the meaning of body in the context of Jesus' teaching on the unity and indissolubility of marriage (particularly in reference to Matt. 19:3ff). When queried about his position on divorce, Jesus responded within the context of the 'beginning.' John Paul II said, '"The beginning" means, therefore, that which the Book of Genesis speaks about. It is, therefore, Genesis 1:27 that Christ quotes, in summary form: "In the beginning the Creator made them male and female."'[8] In Audiences focused on the original unity of man and woman, John Paul II repeatedly spoke of the essential meaning of the body. For example, he noted:

Man, whom God created 'male and female,' bears the divine image imprinted on his body 'from the beginning': man and woman constitute, as it were, two different ways of the human 'being a body' in the unity of that image. Now, it is opportune to turn again to those fundamental words which Christ used, that is, the word 'created' and the subject 'Creator', introducing in the considerations made so far a new dimension, a new criterion of understanding and interpretation which we will call 'hermeneutics of the gift.'[9]

It is the 'gift' dimension that determines the crucial truth and

[8] Pope John Paul II, *Original Unity of Man and Woman*, p. 17.
[9] Pope John Paul II, *Original Unity of Man and Woman*, p. 102.

depth-meaning of 'original solitude-unity-nakedness,' said John Paul. In this way one reaches the 'heart' of creation's mystery, enabling the construction of a Theology of the Body.

PERFECT FULFILLMENT OF EMBODIMENT IN CHRIST

It was in Christ, the eternal Word made flesh, that the redemptive, embodied expression of the human vocation to be living icon of God came to its fullest realization. Through his life, teaching and redemptive Self-gift there was a possibility of entering anew the mystery of being embodied image of God. Cipriano Vagaggini stresses the permanent and universal mediation of Jesus Christ in restoring humanity's vocation. His resurrected, glorified body 'continues to play the same role that the body in general has in the person and activity of a man.'[10] Since the function of the body in human nature has so often been scorned in favor of the soul, says Vagaggini:

> We therefore no longer understand how within the means of salvation willed by God the physical body of Christ possesses a function *that is always active and permanent and even eternal.* Consequently we no longer clearly see the function of the resurrection of Christ – and therefore that of the paschal mystery and of our own resurrection – nor the function of the eucharistic mystery.[11]

The *reality* and *permanent* effectiveness of Christ's body has direct bearing upon a faith understanding of body-meaning. In fact, Theology of the Body hinges on the manner in which Incarnation is interpreted. In the latter half of the twentieth century theologians have openly debated the value of maintaining the understanding of the Incarnation received in the Christian tradition. In the 1970s Maurice Wiles, for example, suggested that the Incarnation could be interpreted in two ways. The 'looser meaning,' he said, 'characterizes Christianity as a religion in which man's approach to God is through the physical world

[10] Cipriano Vagaggini, *The Flesh*, p. 43.
[11] Cipriano Vagaggini, *The Flesh*, p. 16.

rather than by escape from it.'[12] On the other hand, the 'narrower meaning' of the Incarnation describes Christianity as a faith 'whose central tenet affirms the incarnation of God in the particular individual Jesus of Nazareth.'[13] Wiles suggests that the narrower meaning is no longer essential and that it is possible to have 'Christianity' without the traditional understanding of Jesus Christ's true Incarnation in the flesh. This deft division in incarnational meanings impacts not only the identity of Christ, but also the *meaning* of human embodiment in itself. Every mystery of Christian faith is affirmed or denied in terms of it, from Christ's birth of the Virgin Mary, to his Revelation of inner trinitarian life, his bodily resurrection and his Real Presence in the Eucharist. The genuineness and the intrinsic meaning of Christ's embodiment touches each of the central tenets of faith. There is currently a tendency in the West to reduce the 'historical Jesus' to an indefinite figure (the media, at times, further reduces his identity to that of a misguided zealot, or a profligate who had sexual misadventures). Dissociation of Jesus Christ from the reality of historical existence in the flesh undermines every aspect of Christian faith.

As discussed in Chapter One, the New Testament already was responding to various Docetic and Gnostic denials of Jesus Christ's real embodiment. The majestic Prologue to John's Gospel proclaims the early Church's faith in the reality and effective *meaning* of the Incarnation. It gathers all creation into the mystery of Incarnation. The Gospel writer opens the proclamation in a manner parallel to Genesis: 'In the beginning. . . .' The Word, with God from the beginning, who *was* God before the universe was created, and through whom it received its existence, became *flesh* (*sarx*) and lived, dwelt among us, says John:

> He was in the world
> that had its being through him,
> and the world did not know him.
> He came to his own domain
> and his own people did not accept him.
> But to all who did accept him

[12] Maurice Wiles, 'Christianity Without Incarnation?' in *The Myth of God Incarnate*, ed. John Hick (Philadelphia, 1977), p. 1.
[13] Maurice Wiles, 'Christianity Without Incarnation?' p. 1.

> he gave power to become children of God,
> to all who believe in the name of him
> who was born not out of human stock
> or urge of the flesh
> or will of man
> but of God himself.
> The Word was made flesh,
> he lived among us,
> and we saw his glory,
> the glory that is his as the only Son of the Father,
> full of grace and truth (Jn. 1:10–14).

In poetic, liturgical language, the Gospel writer declares the dignity of Jesus' human embodiment and the consummate realization of the human vocation in the Word made flesh. The initial verses of 1 John are a further emphatic assertion of the reality of Christ's flesh, reiterating that the subject, the Person of whom John writes, not only existed 'since the beginning' but also was a living person whom his early followers had seen and watched, whom they had heard and touched with their own hands (see 1 Jn. 1:1–3).

Theological queries about the reality of Jesus Christ's embodiment, then, are not novel to the twentieth century. They were already rife among Docetists and Gnostics. There are two predominant circumstances that bring new dimensions to contemporary questioning of Christ's bodily reality: 1) what might be termed the 'stance' of those who question; and 2) the manner in which mass media communicates information concerning incarnational issues. First, prior to the Enlightenment, theology was basically approached from a stance of faith. Research, reflection and writing were predominantly the work of those committed to seeking a deeper understanding of the faith they professed. Theological study and writing were mainly carried out in the early Church by bishops who bore a particular responsibility for the 'deposit of faith.' As social conditions changed in the Middle Ages it was monastics (women as well as men) who maintained a strong theological presence. When universities became centers of learning and inquiry in thirteenth-century Europe, women were not admitted either to learn or to teach, and opportunities for women's contributions, or active theological dialogue between women and men diminished sharply. Even during the period of the Enlightenment and its aftermath, however, many who pursued theological study did so from a faith-stance. Only in the twentieth century was there a radical departure from that understanding of theological endeavor.

Today it is possible to discern at least three stances among those who pursue basic theological questions: first, those who practice theology as an academic profession, prizing an objectivity that does not require personal commitment; second, those who continue to carry out theological work from a faith-stance; and third, those who pursue theology from a revisionist stance. While all may deal with similar areas of research and discussion, presuppositions and principles from which their work proceeds will be radically different. This is certainly the case with core issues concerning the meaning of embodiment. The reality of Jesus Christ, the Word made flesh, is the hinge for interpreting and understanding familiar New Testament issues: 'She will give birth to a son and you must name him Jesus because he is the one who is to save his people from their sins' (Matt. 1:21); 'Who do people say the Son of Man is?' (Matt. 16:14); 'The Word was made flesh, he lived among us...' (Jn. 1:14); 'He is not here, for he has risen, as he said he would' (Matt. 28:6). What Pheme Perkins says of the early Christian response to Gnosticism applies to the present:

> Responding to gnostic challenges led christian writers to insist upon the humanity of Jesus, the effectiveness of his death as atonement, the resurrection of the body, the adequacy of the canonical writings as revelation, the effectiveness of the sacraments, and the possibility of salvation for all believers rather than of the elite who possessed 'knowledge.'[14]

THE EMBODIED VOCATION: TO BE IN THE IMAGE OF THE TRIUNE GOD

As we have seen, the Priestly account of creation in Genesis presumes that the vocation to be in the image and likeness of God

---

[14] Pheme Perkins, 'Gnosticism,' in *The New Dictionary of Theology*, ed. Joseph A. Komonchak, *et al* (Wilmington, DE, 1987), p. 423.

involves the integral unity of the body-person. Further, the meaning of human embodiment has been realized in its full potential in the Incarnate Word. Although the concrete details are unique for each human being, there are three characteristics of the human vocation that are manifest in and through the Incarnation: 1) the call to be image and likeness of God is realized in and through the body; 2) it is a call to inter-personal communion; and 3) the destiny of the lived body is resurrected life.

Although the Hebrew Scriptures strongly affirmed that, from human origins, woman and man were to image God, it was only in divine Self-revelation in Jesus Christ that the One God manifested divine identity as a communion of Persons. The supreme Revelation of God's inner life occurred in Jesus' Last Discourse. During his public life he had frequently spoken of his intimate union with the Father, and the synoptic writers, as well as John, write of the Spirit's collaborative presence with him, beginning with his conception in Mary's womb through the overshadowing of the Spirit. At the Last Supper, however, there is the fullest Revelation of divine inner life, together with Christ's explicit invitation that his followers participate in it and know the pattern of it in their relations with him and one another. The Discourse interweaves prayer to the Father with tender counsel for his own: 'Holy Father, keep those you have given me true to your name, so that they may be one like us.... May they all be one. Father, may they be one in us, as you are in me and I am in you' (Jn. 17:11, 21). There is repeated reference to his sending the Spirit, 'another Advocate to be with you forever, that Spirit of truth whom the world can never receive since it neither sees nor knows him; but you know him, because he is with you, he is in you' (Jn. 14:16–17). Jesus speaks with familiar intensity of a way of being that is simultaneously an enduring indwelling presence, and a dynamic interpenetration. In the early centuries of Christian reflection on Jesus' Revelation concerning God's inner life, theologians came to speak of the Trinity, or the triune God, and the Greek term they chose to express the twofold dynamic of indwelling and interpenetration of Persons was *perichoresis*. Leonardo Boff explains:

> Its first meaning is that of being contained in another, dwelling in, being in another – a situation, a state of fact.... Applied to the

mystery of the communion of the Trinity this signified: one Person is in the others, surrounds the others on all sides.... Its second meaning is active and signifies the interpenetration or interweaving of one Person with the others and in the others. This understanding seeks to express the living and eternal process of relating intrinsic to the three Persons, so that each is always penetrating the others.[15]

It is in the context of a final meal, after washing his apostles' feet, and handing over to them his own body and blood in Self-gift that he reveals the inner relations of God. He promised that the Spirit of Truth whom he would send from the Father would bring to their minds what he had told them. As the *Catechism of the Catholic Church* states, the Trinity is the core mystery in the hierarchy of the truths of faith. The One God whom embodied persons are to image is a Trinity of Persons. How can this be? To image God is to participate in the mystery of perichoresis as an embodied person. Part of the difficulty in seeking understanding is that the mystery of the Trinity has been highly intellectualized. Colin Gunton notes that Western Christianity has had the tendency to treat the doctrine of the Trinity as a problem 'rather than as encapsulating the heart of the Christian Gospel,'[16] and he holds St. Augustine especially responsible for this. Using citations from Augustine's *De trinitate* to illustrate this thesis, Gunton identifies three tendencies toward intellectualism: 1) Augustine's manner of hierarchizing analogies most suitable for the Trinity, finding those least suitable that contain any element of materiality and specifying that the image is most apparent in man according to the mind, '*secundum mentem*' (see XV. 5); 2) Augustine tended to think of a God in terms of a 'supermind,' with knowledge being the dominant category in his discussion of divine inner life (see XV. 23); and 3) his moving away from concrete materiality in discussing *word* (see XV. 20) so that the Eternal Word is seen 'as *abstract*, rather than the concrete person of the Son in relation to the Father and Spirit.'[17] The familiar and

---

[15] Leonardo Boff, *Trinity and Society*, trans. Paul Burns (Maryknoll, NY, 1988), pp. 135-136.
[16] Colin E. Gunton, *The Promise of Trinitarian Theology* (Edinburgh, 1991), p. 31.
[17] Colin Gunton, *The Promise of Trinitarian Theology*, p. 44. For a more thorough analysis of Augustine's influence see the entire chapter, pp. 31-57.

predominant analogy that Augustine uses for inner trinitarian life is the inner structure of the human 'mind' with its threefold powers of intellect, memory and will.

Three problems arise if this analogy is over-stressed: 1) the whole mental triad is situated in one person; 2) in being attributed to the 'mind,' the three lack reference to the whole embodied person; and 3) they lack relationship beyond the individual. No analogy is perfect, and each that bears a significant correlation adds to a greater understanding. Despite the inadequacies of Augustine's ground-breaking efforts to deepen understanding of trinitarian life, he laid foundations for further use of analogies in contemplating divine inner life. It is to Augustine that we owe the dictum that *all of creation bears 'vestiges' of the Trinity*. All creatures (as varied as they are) sign the trinitarian Creator in some way, with humans specifically called to be 'image.'

Certainly a major obstacle in seeing humanity in the image of trinitarian life comes from placing the similarity in *nature* rather than *person* – or, as just discussed, in seeing likeness only in the inner faculties of the human person – by-passing the bodilyness and materiality. Only when the Second Person of the Trinity became incarnate and lived as all humans do could the complete Revelation occur concerning God's inner life, inviting for all time a pondering of the revelatory passage of Genesis 1:27: 'God created man in the image of himself, in the image of God he created him, male and female he created them.' This will have bearing on each succeeding chapter of this book since all Theology of the Body is rooted in the core mysteries of the Trinity, the Incarnation, and the vocation to be image of God. When Augustine discerned that all of creation bears 'vestiges' of the Trinity, he could not have known the multiple ways in which this could be recognized even in the minuscule material aspects of embodiment. Theologically, we are only at the beginning of correlating the insights of the life sciences with the core doctrines of the faith. How much remains to be appropriated in the brief statement: *male and female he created them*. The awakening which has occurred since the 1960s concerning women's bodies, and the intense questioning of interrelationships among men and women have opened Theology of the Body with a force comparable to the release of atomic energy in the realm of physics. As in the case of nuclear energy, there are as yet no adequate ways of ensuring

that the explosive energy generated by the Women's Move-
ment(s) of the latter twentieth century can be adequately enfleshed without an uncontainable explosive force. Initial probes
in the immense issue of male-female relationship are beginning to
yield theological insight. In summarizing the creation accounts of
Genesis, Mary Aquin O'Neill notes how human existence is
recognized as a divine *gift* that is accompanied with the responsibility of ruling over all other created beings. Being created in the
image and likeness of God, she says, means knowing 'one's self as
male or female only in the presence of the sexually differentiated
other' and knowing 'that one's rule is limited, bound by the
command of God. From the beginning, then, the image of God is
reflected in a community of persons, in a humankind that is
created male and female.... Humankind is "image," not very
God.'[18]

TRINITARIAN PATTERNS PERVADE HUMAN LIFE AND ALL CREATION

The 'vestiges' of trinitarian life pervade all of creation. *Every
truth of being that reveals itself contributes to a faith understanding of embodiment and matter.* This concerns the body
itself from the very early stages of human existence. Until
recently it was thought that the earliest cell divisions within the
zona pellucida (the membrane that surrounds the embryo)
always occurred in multiples of two. Now it is known that in the
first division, one cell splits first and the other 'waits.' There is a
three-cell-stage.

Geneticist Dr. Jerome Lejeune noted that the DNA received
from the mother for differentiation in cell development is
'marked' on a different place from that contributed by the father.
The first cell to divide begins to build the body of the child (it
bears the female 'mark'); the second cell, as it divides, initiates the
containing 'envelope' which protects the earliest stages of the
child (it bears the male 'mark'). At the sixteen-cell stage there is a

---

[18] Mary Aquin O'Neill, 'The Mystery of Being Human Together,' in *Freeing Theology: The Essentials of Theology in Feminist Perspective*, ed. Catherine Mowry
LaCugna (San Francisco, 1993), p. 141.

great compaction within the protective envelope, or *zona pellucida*. *Three* cells within its center are compacted by those surrounding them. Speaking figuratively, Lejeune said that as the three in the middle become compacted they 'talk to one another.' It is as if they 'decide they'll work together' to build the body, while the outer cells are building membrane and placenta to protect the new human being.[19] There is a trinitarian pattern in this very elemental stage of human life, said Lejeune. According to him, it would be impossible to clone a human being by replacing the nucleus of a cell taken at random from the body. Chromosomes from one sex can be induced to form tumors, or growths that repeat a certain kind of cell, but *two* sexes are required for the combined information that constitutes the first cell's 'inner dialogue.' From that union 'the first cell knows all. It knows how to build a human being.' The very structures of the embryonic human body – whether it is conceived within marital covenant, or technically 'produced' in a laboratory dish – are marked with a trinitarian pattern and are enfleshed through the complementary male-female genetic heritage. The *meaning* of human embodiment is already physically inscribed in the minuscule beginnings of life, prior to any individual's conscious realization. Body development itself signs the vocation to be image and likeness of God and to live in union. The *truth* so cryptically present in that beginning is present throughout life: the vocation to be image of the trinitarian communion of Persons.

The genetic pattern concretized in the *zona pellucida* is like a map whose effectiveness does not depend upon size but on the truth of its intricate patterning. Even a small world map can contain the basic pattern of the world, allowing one to visualize relationships among oceans and continents, to study the names and terrains of distant lands familiar to ancestors, and to plan future journeys across the earth. So, too, the micro beginnings of embodied life encompass the patterns of the unique person, created in divine and human relationship. In this case, the developing body-person *is* its own living map, relating to the pattern of the entire universe within trinitarian relationship. It is the unique, living pattern received totally as gift from the collabora-

---

[19] See Dr. Jerome Lejeune, 'Biological Happening or a Future for Mankind?' McGivney Lecture, October 29, 1993.

tion of Creator and parents that makes it possible for any human person (without losing his/her identity) to be a 'crossing point' where the entire universe can dynamically participate in conscious wonder, praise and thanks – in a freely chosen response to the divine offer of relationship. The body is a living crossroad within the created universe, a midway point between distant galaxies and the unimaginably minute subatomic 'particles' in the nucleus of an atom. Teilhard de Chardin observed: *'My matter is not a part of the universe that I possess totaliter. It is the totality of the universe that I possess partialiter.'*[20]

The insights received through contemporary research in physics and the life sciences suggest a deepened theological significance in Jesus' call to 'take up his cross and follow me' (Mk. 8:34). Every member of the human family is a 'living cross-ing' within creation. The lived body is a cross-ing point of the material universe, so that within the conscious imaging of God, all of material creation can be 'taken up' into a redemptive union with Jesus Christ. 'Taking up one's cross' in the present era of history involves a conscious awareness of responsibility for stewardship in ways that surpass all former understandings of stewardship and the body itself as cross-ing point. The earth (one small, dense knot of dynamic matter within the universe) is entrusted to human stewardship not first in its immensity, but primarily in the unique synthesis of each 'I-body' received within the dynamics of conscious bodily existence. The extent to which any individual's body is received and cared for as gift (or disdained, rejected, simply 'used') already determines the manner in which the world-encompassing mandate of Genesis is realized or abandoned:

'Let us make man in our own image, in the likeness of ourselves, and let them be masters of the fish of the sea, the birds of heaven, the cattle, all the wild beasts and all the reptiles that crawl upon the earth'.... God blessed them, saying to them, 'Be fruitful, multiply, fill the earth and conquer it. Be masters of the fish of the sea, the birds of heaven and all living animals on the earth.' God said, 'See, I give you all the seed-bearing plants that are upon the

[20] Pierre Teilhard de Chardin, 'En quoi consiste le corps humain?' in *Science et Christ* (Paris: Editions du Seuil, 1965), p. 34. Quoted portion trans. by Sister M. Timothy Prokes.

whole earth, and all the trees with seed-bearing fruit; this shall be your food'.... And so it was. God saw all he had made, and indeed it was very good (Gen. 1:26; 28–31).

Lejeune alluded also to the 'vestiges' of trinitarian patterning in other living creatures, noting what has been learned from experiments with mice in their early cell development. Through laboratory experimentation it was found that portions of mouse cells could be replaced and recombined at the eight and sixteen-cell stages. Black and white strains were combined, yielding a checkered fur. A third color was introduced, now yielding a tri-colored fur. When experimenters tried to induce a fourth color of mouse, however, they found it could not be done: they had exceeded the limit. Reflecting on this information, Lejeune said that the mouse is 'telling itself at the three-cell stage: "we are *not* a population of cells; we are bound to be a mouse."'[21] It was not possible to compact more than three lines. 'We learned that individuality was a kind of trinary system. We need to have three cells talking to one another to decide, "I am an individual."'[22]

Previous to such insights from the life sciences, it would not have seemed appropriate to see trinitarian vestiges in these genetic patternings. Lejeune's observations invite further theological reflection on the manner in which resonances of divine life are found in other life-forms. The recurring but distorted urge to make aspects of creation into gods and goddesses is explicable in light of the genuine human vocation to center all creation in conscious, love-response to the divine personal Trinity. To treat any creature as a divinity is to deflect it from its divine source and leave it stranded in a non-integral cul-de-sac. Recent scientific endeavors not only open new avenues for exploring the meaning of 'taking up one's cross' but also for receiving anew Paul's saying: 'From the beginning till now the entire creation, as we know, has been groaning in one great act of giving birth; and not only creation, but all of us who possess the first-fruits of the Spirit, we too groan inwardly as wait for our bodies to be set free' (Rom. 8:22–23). Paul does not advocate an attempt to be freed from the body. Rather, he says that 'our bodies' (that is, the visible expression of living persons) are to be set free. Later

---

[21] Jerome Lejeune, 'Biological Happening or a Future for Mankind?'
[22] Jerome Lejeune, 'Biological Happening or a Future for Mankind?'

chapters will probe the meaning of Paul's affirmation in light of the resurrection of Christ and the Assumption of Mary, Mother of God. The human body-person is destined for a transformed transcendence. Paul links groaning and birthing within the larger creation to the freedom of lived bodies. All authentic ecological concerns are concrete expressions of the vocation to stewardship. Concern for the fulfillment of creation differs substantially from survival strategy, or from creating unfettered programs of innovation which result from hubris. Before seeing how the embodied vocation to personal communion and stewardship is expressed in ordinary presence to one another, in the lived experiences of sexuality, work, worship, suffering and death, it will be necessary to consider the lived body as participant in the mystery of Revelation.

6

Body as Revelatory

To be embodied is to participate in the mystery of Revelation, of self-manifestation. It will be the work of this chapter to consider what that means concretely within a Theology of the Body. The term 'revelation' (literally 'to unveil') means to make known. Christianity is one of the three world religions that is designated a 'revealed religion' (the other two being Judaism and Islam). Even among Christian theologians, however, the *meaning* of Revelation is not understood univocally, and different aspects of it have been emphasized during the history of the Church. New Testament writings emphasized the immediacy of personal Revelation in Jesus Christ, with the writer of Matthew's Gospel particularly showing how he fulfilled what was fore-shadowed in the Old Testament. At times during the past two millennia, greater emphasis has been placed on Revelation as *'inner illumination'* or divine teaching; at other times the stress has been on informational *content* which has been received through perceivable, historical events. In certain periods the term has been applied especially to *propositions* formulated in order to hand on core Revelation. In recent theologizing there has been a shift from a *propositional* to a more *personal* understanding of Revelation:

> Revelation is now understood fundamentally as God's *self*-rev-elation. It is first of all the gift of God's own being, and only secondly is it the illuminative or propositional unfolding of the foundational event of a divine self-giving.[1]

Revelation differs from the process of discovery and from knowledge gained through careful scrutiny of data. 'Revelation,' like many other words which connote sacred realities, has been

---

[1] John F. Haught, 'Revelation,' in *The New Dictionary of Theology*, p. 884.

exploited in commercial advertising and the entertainment media in which 'revelation' often suggests the exposition of scandalous information. In faith understanding, *Revelation* means primarily divine Personal Self-disclosure of God's inner life, made known in a consummate manner in the Incarnate Word. As Rahner affirms, divine Self-manifestation simultaneously illumines the meaning of human existence and the vocation of all creation. Revelation in this fundamental sense cannot be conjured, earned or forced. It is a gift to be recognized and received. The Scriptures indicate that primordial Revelation was given unexpectedly, in ways transcending human calculations, often overcoming seeming impossibilities. God's Self-manifestation exceeds human control and evokes (in Rudolph Otto's well-known terminology) both *fascination* and *awe*. This is a pervasive theme of both Old and New Testaments. Cogent accounts of Revelation given to Abraham, Moses, and the major prophets bear testimony to the experience of fascination and awe in those who were recipients of it. They knew both holy fear and attentive receptivity for the revealing Presence.

The Hebrew people described God's activity in history as *dabar*, meaning a 'word-event.' Divine Self-disclosure was never given merely for the sake of conveying information: it was a form of Self-gift expressed in a manner that embodied humans could apprehend sensibly in the 'here and now,' but which exceeded ordinary limits of space and time. *Dabar* meant an efficacious word, accomplishing what it communicated. As humanity grew in its capacity to perceive and respond to divine Self-manifestation, even in an elementary manner, God disclosed aspects of what it means for 'God to be God' and what it means for humanity to be brought into redemptive relationship. In the fullness of time, when there had been sufficient preparation, the completely efficacious Word was *disclosed in the flesh*: ultimate Revelation has been given in the Person of the eternal Word made man. Everything necessary for human salvation has been efficaciously disclosed in a gift that is everlasting – for all peoples of the earth at all moments of history. Divine Revelation to humanity has taken place in the space-time material universe and the Scriptures are particularly graphic in detailing the *embodied* experience of receiving it. Primordial Revelation occurred in the midst of daily events: to Abraham when he welcomed visitors; to

Moses as he tended sheep; and to Mary as she anticipated married life in the village of Nazareth. Despite the abundance of scriptural evidence, the concept of divine Revelation occurring within a particular time and place, and to specific, historical persons constitutes a major difficulty for some theologians (reflecting secular society's difficulty with recognizing transcendent mysteries of faith as these are expressed in concrete and particularized circumstances). Belief that the divine Word became enfleshed as a Jewish male who worked at the trade of an ordinary Galilean, and used the imagery of a naïve world-view, constitutes a 'scandal of particularity' for many.

Hebrews 5 links Jesus' human experiences, particularly his suffering, with the efficaciousness of his being 'high priest.' It states that he was 'taken out of mankind' to act for humanity in relation to God, being able to sympathize with the ignorant and uncertain 'because he too lives in the limitations of weakness' (Heb. 5:2). Poignantly, the author of Hebrews says: 'During his life on earth, he offered up prayer and entreaty, aloud and in silent tears, to the one who had the power to save him out of death, and he submitted so humbly that his prayer was heard. Although he was Son, he learnt to obey through suffering ...' (5:7–9). Precisely because he was truly enfleshed, he could translate *bodily* both divine Presence and saving Self-gift. The priests of the covenant with Israel repeated sacrifices daily, but these were incapable of taking away sin. In the Hebrew covenant, only the high priest could enter the inner sanctuary of the temple, the Holy of Holies, once a year. Hebrews 10 contrasts the ineffectiveness of the old sacrifices with the efficacious, once-for-all sacrifice of Christ. Through Jesus' blood, says Hebrews, we have the 'right' to enter the sanctuary 'by a new way which he has opened for us, a living opening through the curtain, that is to say, his body' (10:19–20). Hebrews attributes a prayer to Christ in which he says on coming into the world that God did not want sacrifice or oblation, but 'prepared a body for me' (10:5). The text reiterates his cry, 'Here I am!' come to do your will. '... and this *will* was for us to be made holy by the *offering* of his *body* made once and for all by Jesus Christ' (10:10).

Christ came as efficacious disclosure of God within the realities of embodied life: he spoke as Galileans did, wept, cried out, and relished food. He grew up with the restrictions of a village carpenter. The 'curtain' of his body was 'a living opening' into universal redemption. The curtain metaphor employed by the author of Hebrews is apt. *Revelation* does not imply a total clarity of understanding: while it reveals, it simultaneously conceals the depths of personal mystery.

It is a mark of authentic personal love that every self-disclosure elicits an increased capacity on the part of the beloved to recognize a further, previously unguessed horizon of personal mystery. In Christ, the divine plan of salvation was personally, bodily effected on earth in a manner perceptible to those who witnessed it (see 1 John). Jesus' Last Discourse made explicit his mission of manifesting his Father and inner trinitarian life. It was through bodily perceivable words and actions that he disclosed God. While divine Revelation is an effective word, it is offered, not imposed. There is no certainty that it will be received *as* Revelation. (When transmitted through the living tradition of faith, divine Self-disclosure has been ignored, misinterpreted, rejected, and utilized for personal gain.) More than a conveying of information, Revelation is Self-manifestation of a divine communion of Persons, inviting response from those who receive it. The multiple accounts of those who were recipients of Revelation (whether in Old or New Covenants) shows how their lives were changed by it. They came to recognize that it was not for their personal consolation or aggrandizement. Rather, it incorporated a mission to be fulfilled for the sake of the whole people. There was fear, even terror, in those who recognized that they were being visited by a Self-disclosing God. *They found that in receiving divine Self-manifestation, they, too, were disclosed, known to the depths of their being.* Their sinfulness and unworthiness were exposed to them through the God who addressed them in some manner in a mysterious, loving, unfathomable Presence. From Abraham, through Isaiah and Peter, there was an instinctual dread before the immediacy of the divine which required *everything* of them and affected all humanity.

The recipients of primordial divine Revelation were able to recognize and receive it because it was given in a manner accommodated to their bodilyness. This is clear 'from the beginning' as Pope John Paul II notes in his series of public Audiences on Genesis 1–3. The chronologically earlier creation account of Genesis (Gen. 2–3), anthropomorphically describing the creation of Adam and Eve, is graphically corporeal. As a theological narrative, it accounts for divine creativity in the language of dust, breath, a rib, and the eating of forbidden fruit. *From 'the beginning' it is clear that human persons participate in the mystery of Revelation in and through their bodilyness.* In the Yahwist narrative, God is portrayed as fashioning the beasts and birds and bringing them to 'Adam' to see what he would name them. The text reveals clear recognition of the distinction between human and animal life, a realization of human uniqueness among all other created beings, a realization that John Paul II calls 'original human solitude.' He notes that this passage in the Yahwist narrative precedes the portion concerning the creation of Eve and it is in reference to the solitude of the human being as such, and not just the male.[2] Analysis of the Yahwist account of the 'beginning,' says John Paul, allows us to link the meaning of original solitude with conscious awareness of the meaning of body through which one *is* person. Bodily structure allows one to be author of genuine human activity, and it is on the basis of body and not simply self-awareness and self-determination that one is a 'subject.' Commenting on the male-man's 'awakening from genetic sleep' in recognition of the female ('This at last is bone from my bones, and flesh from my flesh! This is to be called woman, for this was taken from man' – Gen. 2:23.) John Paul says: 'Exclaiming in this way, he seems to say: here is *a body that expresses the "person"!'*[3]

We have seen that divine Revelation is given to human persons in their bodilyness, and it attained its supreme expression in and through the embodied Word. To be created in body, in the image and likeness of God, is already a participation in the mystery of personal Revelation. In order to see this foundational principle of Theology of the Body more clearly, it is necessary to see *how body is symbol.* This will further enable an understanding of 1) human sexuality; 2) the human vocation to be a communion of persons; and 3) the dignity of human work, communication, suffering, and death.

[2] See John Paul II, *Original Unity of Man and Woman*, p. 44, and f.n. 1: 'The Hebrew text constantly calls the first man *ha-'adam*, while the term *'is* ('male') is introduced only when contrasted with *'issa* ('female'). So 'man' was solitary without reference to sex' (p. 48).

[3] John Paul II, *Original Unity of Man and Woman*, p. 109.

BODY AS REVELATORY SYMBOL

The familiar word 'symbol' bears numerous connotations and denotations. It will be necessary to specify its meaning here, in regard to a theological understanding of the body. Arthur Vogel reminds us that the lived body is meaningful to us and is the source of our finding meaning in other things because it locates our presence. 'Personal presence is more than the body, but we are able to know it to be more only through the body and never without a body.'[4] Even when employed in regard to the human body, the term *symbol* still bears a variety of meanings. William van Roo says that there is no single criterion that suffices for classifying symbols,[5] but he proposes two general classes: external and internal symbols. Among the internal symbols are the images found in our perceiving, remembering, imagining and dreaming – as well as those images (often only half-formed) that are integral to conceptualizing, reasoning and making judgments: '... there is no thought without symbolization, the formation of a meaningful sensuous element.'[6] Other internal symbols are those found in our emotions, will acts and motor impulses. Our personal body image itself encompasses a whole area of internal symbols, says van Roo. There are sensuous factors in our own condition of being in the world that are significant because they provide bearing and context in a 'field' of relationships. Each throb of pain, for example, can be 'an ironic symbol of human fragility: how little it takes to hobble a man!'[7]

Among the *external* symbols enumerated by van Roo are 1) such elementary ones as facial expression and gesture; 2) vocal and instrumental sounds; 3) those symbols wrought by shaping external matter and those *developed* for functional and communication purposes (language, speech, artistic and dramatic

---

[4] Arthur Vogel, *Body Theology*, p. 91.
[5] See William van Roo, *Man the Symbolizer* (Rome: Gregorian University Press, 1981), p. 217. He says: 'Symbolizing is properly human, and symbols are human works. They are the immediate terms of human intentional acts: immediate, not ultimate, since they are intended somehow to affect the worlds in which men and women operate. They are sensuous, for they are part of the mystery of humanly bodily meaning.' p. 221.
[6] William van Roo, *Man the Symbolizer*, p. 225.
[7] William van Roo, *Man the Symbolizer*, p. 227.

images, and those which express concepts in the sciences); 4) symbols in ordinary life (usually falling short of the formal perfection found in artistic symbols); and 5) religious symbols (particularly those which are 'sacramental').[8]

While van Roo details types of symbols according to internal and external classifications, it is also possible to designate symbols according to a different set of categories: 1) *conventional symbols* (those humanly fashioned and then assigned meanings, such as language, written configurations and signs); 2) *natural symbols* (which innately have meaning across cultures and eras, such as water, earth, air and fire); and 3) *mixed symbols* (which combine natural and conventional meanings, such as bread, wine and oil). Each type of symbol, no matter what system of classification is used, has a 'body base.' It participates in what van Roo says is *'a human work in which the sensuous is somehow meaningful.'*[9]

There is a still more fundamental meaning of symbol, however, that gives foundation and meaning to all the lesser types of symbols cited above. It is what Karl Rahner designates on the ontological level as *Real Symbol*. More than a particular internal human act or an external expression of meaning, Real Symbol indicates a basic constitutive quality of *being* itself. In 'The Theology of the Symbol,' Rahner wrote:

> What then is the primordial meaning of symbol and symbolic, according to which each being is in itself and for itself symbolic, and hence (and to this extent) symbolic for another? It is this: as a being realizes itself in its own intrinsic 'otherness' (which is constitutive of its being), retentive of its intrinsic plurality (which is contained in its self-realization) as its derivative and hence congruous expression, it makes itself known.[10]

What is the meaning of Rahner's densely-packed assertion regarding *symbol in its primordial sense*? He is saying that all being *is* constitutively symbolic, from within its own existence. There is an intrinsic plurality in every being: to 'realize' or *be* itself, each being is *expressed* (what Rahner terms its 'otherness').

[8] See William van Roo, *Man the Symbolizer*, pp. 215–267, for an extended discussion of symbols in their variety.

[9] William van Roo, *Man the Symbolizer*, p. 215.

[10] Karl Rahner, 'The Theology of the Symbol,' in *Theological Investigations*, Vol. IV, trans. Kevin Smyth (London, 1966), p. 231.

This is not something added on, but is rather *constitutive* of any existent being. Through this self-expression it 'makes itself known.' It is this quality of being that Rahner calls 'Real Symbol.' Every other type of symbol, no matter what classification is used, is derived from and extends from this basic meaning.

For the human person, the *body* is the 'Real Symbol' through which the whole person is self-realized and makes itself known. 'The symbol strictly speaking (symbolic reality) is the self-realization of a being in the other, which is constitutive of its essence.'[11] Rahner cites the Trinity as the ontological basis for his assertions about 'Real Symbol,' pointing out that a 'plurality' right within being does not necessarily indicate finiteness or imperfection. *Every being* bears an intrinsic plurality which is not detrimental to its unity and perfection. In fact, it is precisely in the theology of the Logos, the Word, that the theology of symbol is humanly recognized in its supreme form:

> ... the incarnate word is the absolute symbol of God in the world, filled as nothing else can be with what is symbolized. He is not merely the presence and revelation of what God is in himself. He is also the expressive presence of what – or rather, who – God wished to be, in free grace, to the world, in such a way that this divine attitude, once so expressed, can never be reversed, but is and remains final and unsurpassable.[12]

Having located the basic meaning of symbol in the very being of God, Rahner turned to its implications for human embodied life. As has been seen, Real Symbol means a unity of symbol and what is symbolized right from within being itself. This means that individual 'parts' or actions of the person are symbolic of the whole person. There is a unity between what is symbolized and the symbolizer: at the depth of Real Symbol, the symbol contains what it symbolizes. Because there is a wholeness in body-soul being, 'the whole man is somehow present and expressing himself, though the expressive form is confined to start with to one portion of the body.'[13] Each 'part' symbolically bears the func-

---

[11] Karl Rahner, 'The Theology of the Symbol,' p. 234. See also Francis Ryan, *The Body as Symbol: Merleau-Ponty and Incarnational Theology* (Washington, D.C., 1970).
[12] Karl Rahner, 'The Theology of the Symbol,' p. 237.
[13] Karl Rahner, 'The Theology of the Symbol,' p. 248.

tion and force of the whole body-person, although there are degrees of greater or less significance. For this reason, when an organ or part of the body is designated (such as the 'heart' or 'head') in a symbolic sense, it represents the whole person. At the level of Real Symbol, the symbol *is* the reality and from within the integral unity of being, proclaims and reveals the symbolizer. This has immense implications for understanding the dignity of all that is expressed bodily, especially in light of humanity being created in the image of the Trinity, and attaining its perfection in the Incarnate Word. 'Reality and its appearance in the flesh are for ever one in Christianity, inconfused and inseparable.'[14]

THEOLOGICAL 'KNOWING BY HEART'

To designate the body as revelatory means, first of all, that from within the totality of the individual, the living body (Real Symbol) manifests the whole person. In the sense of *dabar*, each person is spoken into being by God; each is called to be an effective word or message of love in the world. That is why Arthur Vogel describes bodies as 'meaning in matter,' as location of body-presence, allowing us to mean what we say and say what we mean. Each human being is a visible word spoken in body and blood. All orally spoken words, all words written by hand, all words that skim electronically at the speed of light are derived from the living body that is *the* message. Every person is uniquely flesh made word, communicating a meaning that is written bodily into a people, a place, and a moment of history. That is why all theology needs to be a 'Theology of the Body,' not simply an intellectual activity. If removed from the bodiedness of Christian life, theology becomes simply an intellectual pursuit, an academic analysis and interpretation of doctrines, praxis, worship and writings.

Pondering the mystery of enfleshed humanity is the entry point for theological reflection on the mystery of God. Rahner described the Incarnate Christ as 'the abbreviated Word of God.' In fact, if God truly became man and remains forever so, 'theology is therefore eternally an anthropology.' Humanity participates in

---

[14] Karl Rahner, 'The Theology of the Symbol,' p. 252.

and articulates the mystery of God.[15] We are forbidden to belittle the human person because to do so would be to belittle God.

Terrence G. Kardong touches upon this in his description of early monastic *lectio divina*, the contemplative pondering of Scripture, practiced in Benedictine monasteries. Kardong says that while we cannot know precisely how this was originally done, *lectio divina* can be described as a rumination (or a 'chewing on the text') so as to incorporate the Word of God into life. Not being speed-readers, early monastics normally read aloud and memorized texts so that they might ruminate upon them during the singing of the Divine Office or recite them in mantra-fashion during manual work. The Word of God evoked a divine-human dialogue. *Lectio* is not to be confused with 'aloof, objective, scientific study' says Kardong. It should open to the most intense and personal of human activities, prayer. The articulated text tends to engrave itself on the heart. Egyptian monks, says Kardong, called scriptural texts which they had memorized their 'by heart.' The Word of God was meant to be heard and spoken, not merely silently seen.[16]

What Kardong describes is a personal, dialogical way of 'knowing' that integrates what is known so that mind, mouth and muscle participate in it. The expression 'to chew on the text' is apt because it is a way of knowing that nourishes the whole person. Anything studied in this manner is bodily drawn into personal existence. It is a 'by-heart' manner of knowing that simultaneously reveals something of the knower. Children who have not been prematurely deprived of innocent receptivity learn innately in this manner, repeating (often singing) what they have learned, raptly 'taking it in' and bodily expressing it – sometimes through cries of delight, rocking motions, or the spontaneous clasping of their head.

SELF-REVELATION THROUGH GESTURES

Since the whole person is expressed bodily, human gestures (e.g. body motions that communicate ideas, passion, emphasis and

---

[15] See Karl Rahner, 'On the Theology of the Incarnation,' p. 116.
[16] See Terrence G. Kardong, 'Chewing the Text: Early Monastic *Lectio Divina* of the Bible,' *The Canadian Catholic Review*, 11, 10 (November, 1993), p. 8.

intent) are a pre-eminent form of self-revelation. The word 'gesture' (from the Latin *gerare* and *gerere* = to carry, to do) has a twofold meaning: the use of the entire body or a portion of the body to communicate, and the act of 'bearing within.' When there is integrity of body-person, what has come to gestation within is brought to outward expression through appropriate gestures. The hands are particularly associated with the act of gesturing. Edmond Barbotin calls the hand 'an organ of vision without intervening distance.'[17] Hands are the person's physical interface with the rest of creation, allowing the whole person to *be* contacted in the very act of contacting.

Gesture is not limited to the hands. It has been seen that the living body, apart from any specific physical activity, is already a perceptible gesture of divine love and creativity in the world. Ultimately (as will be more extensively discussed later) the fundamental gesture of a human being, made in the image and likeness of God, is to be given and received as gift. When this is brought to conscious expression in prayer it becomes worship, bringing a transcendent meaning to the traditional nuptial affirmation: 'with my body I thee worship.'

Because the 'holy' evokes both awe and attraction, scriptural narratives describe how encounter with the Living God induces spontaneous gestures: shielding one's eyes, declaring unworthiness, falling down in adoration. Along with a keen realization of unworthiness, recipients of Revelation articulated gratitude for divine visitation, but there was no premeditated plan in their gestures. Gradually the believing community formalized those liturgical gestures which could express their communal worship. There are, however, some spontaneous forms of veneration that seem to touch archetypal depths across cultures. One can almost designate such gestures 'natural symbols' since they do not have to be 'learned' when there is intense presence of the holy. Some of these have been formally incorporated in liturgical, sacramental life. The Good Friday commemoration of Christ's passion and death begins with the celebrant silently prostrating. Likewise, ordinands who are about to receive the sacrament of Holy Orders prostrate while the community prays for the assistance of

[17] Edmond Barbotin, *The Humanity of Man*, trans. Matthew J. O'Connell (Maryknoll, NY, 1975), p. 194.

the Communion of Saints in the sacramental marking of a man *in Persona Christi*. Although only a few religious communities retain the practice, a solemn prostration traditionally has preceded the profession of vows.

Bowing, a derivative form of prostration, denotes reverence and a sense of the sacred. Kneeling is an act of deference and vulnerability. Once these gestures are separated from inner intent, they can seem meaningless or even become mockery (as evidenced by the soldiers who entertained themselves by ridiculing Christ through the abuse of sacred gestures). When authentic, gestures have a transformative effect not only for those who live them bodily, but also for those who witness them. Etty Hillesum, a Jewess who died at Auschwitz, exemplified this. In her posthumously published journal, *An Interrupted Life*, Hillesum described her spiritual development in the midst of degrading violence and systematically planned death. She amazed herself in the spontaneous bodily responses that she knew in her growing awareness of God's goodness. She became, she said, 'a kneeler in training,' and found herself bowing in thanks for a swatch of sky or the fragrance of wild jasmine. Ann Belford Ulanov reports how Hillesum would stand protectively behind a weeping woman or a hungry, grieving child, sometimes simply placing her arm about them or gazing into their eyes (since she was unafraid of looking suffering 'straight in the eyes'). As the lives of many saints depict, physical horrors can elicit a countering recognition of the holy, expressed bodily.

While it is not possible to discuss them in any detail here, the phenomena that sometimes accompany mystical experience are instructive concerning bodily participation in intense religious experience. John of the Cross vigorously counseled those he directed to disregard such phenomena lest they 1) mistake the phenomena for the actual personal encounter with God; 2) plateau in self-centered pride at receiving such favors; or 3) succumb to deceptions of the evil spirit. Teresa of Avila, aware of these dangers, nevertheless described her own experience of these phenomena and astutely reflected upon them for the benefit of others. The immediate Presence and activity of divine Persons can be so intense that the living body cannot contain its responses in an accustomed manner. The torque placed upon the whole person stretches its ordinary capacities in a manner that can make the body rigid or impervious to normal stimuli. At times the person levitates despite the normal conditions of gravity. Many who ponder Teresa of Avila's mystical journey through the 'interior castle' are surprised when they read 'the seventh mansion.' The fifth and sixth 'mansions' describe varieties of ecstatic experience, leading the reader to anticipate that the mystical marriage of the seventh mansion will exceed the former two in the intensity and variety of phenomena. According to Teresa, however, her mystical marriage to Christ brought a quieting of extraordinary phenomena. In fact, it brought her to increased daily labor and suffering for the benefit of others. Without directly adverting to it, Teresa's account indicates that authentic response to mystical gifts will gradually bring an integration on all levels of the body-person, not opening to increased physical absorption, but to a greater capacity to share in the efficacious suffering and Self-gift of Christ.

LITURGICAL GESTURES INFLUENCED BY CULTURE

Cultural practices have an influence on liturgical gestures. Among Western nations currently, where individual rights and personal empowerment are especially valued, there is a tendency to avoid those gestures of worship that suggest submission and vulnerability. Contemporary designs for places of worship often eliminate 'kneelers' and priedieus. Forming circles, lifting arms in praise and liturgical dance are preferred forms of bodily involvement in prayer. At times, in the attempt to incorporate cultural emphases, those who prepare liturgical functions eliminate gestures which have what may be called an archetypal significance for expressing worship. Prostration, kneeling and bowing express creatureliness, but they are sometimes replaced by dubious substitutions which are not capable of bearing the significance of the whole person. For example, some local churches substitute the *mandatum* or washing of feet with a mutual hand-washing ritual. While this may be an indication of desire to be of mutual service, it is reductionist, failing to express bodily Jesus' example of serving in the most menial manner. To kneel at another's feet is itself a deferential act. Mutual handwashing may prove to be a more comfortable, even practical exchange, but it is symbolically removed from the actions of Christ at the Last Supper and his counsel that the Twelve wash one another's feet in union with his kenotic love.

Authentic gestures should be capable of expressing the whole person integrally in ways that are appropriate. Where there is integrity of expression there is effectiveness, touching both the one who acts and those who are recipients of the action. Because Jesus Christ's risen body has an enduring reality and meaning, the sacraments not only signify what is being wrought on behalf of recipients, but also bear what they signify: the saving, effective Presence of Christ. He is the paradigm for understanding how the lived body is Real Symbol. It is said that Francis of Assisi invited a brother to accompany him into a town so that they might preach. The two walked silently through the streets and without stopping returned home. The brother asked why they had not preached, but Francis replied: we *did*. Like a procession bearing the Blessed Sacrament, they had moved through the city, their bodies conveying a message and a presence whose effectiveness derived from the gracious Presence of God extending through them. It involved more than good example; it implicated the entirety of their lived bodies.

Theologically, much is to be learned from contemporary scientific disciplines concerning the effect that bodies have on one another across intervening space and time. Rupert Sheldrake's hypothesis of 'Formative Causation,' for example, is helpful here in opening fresh approaches to sacramental life and the Communion of Saints. While Sheldrake tries to account for the very nature of life and the transmission of form, development and behavior in living things (a project outside the scope of this text) his basic hypothesis pertains to the very mystery which St. Francis intuited, not simply as a biological or physical fact, but as a *graced possibility of human embodiment.* Sheldrake proposes the existence of 'morphogenetic fields' which 'impose patterned restrictions on the energetically possible outcomes of physical processes.'[18] He maintains that there are measurable physical

[18] Rupert Sheldrake, *A New Science of Life: The Hypothesis of Formative Causation* (Los Angeles, 1981), p. 13.

'fields' which influence the development of forms in nature. 'Where do they come from?', Sheldrake asks:

> The answer suggested is that they are derived from the morpho-genetic fields associated with previous similar systems: the mor-phogenetic fields of all past systems become *present* to any subsequent similar system; the structures of past systems affect subsequent similar systems by a cumulative influence which acts across both space *and time*.[19]

The hypothesis of formative causation suggests that events occurring in one part of the world may induce the same type of effect elsewhere without any *known* physical connection or com-munication. Previous patterns seem to have a causal influence that is trans-spatial and trans-temporal. The only way this can be discussed, says Sheldrake, is by way of analogy. The most appro-priate *physical* analogy, he says, is that of *resonance*, which means that a system can be acted upon by an alternating force when both share a coinciding 'natural frequency of vibration.'[20] The familiar act of tuning a radio to a specific frequency vibra-tion illustrates this basic principle. No matter how complex the number of vibrational patterns passing through a room, when a radio transmission is received, there is a selective attunement to a particular vibration. In Sheldrake's theory, there is a three-dimensional influence of 'past forms' on present ones, resonating with them. Our interest here is not in Sheldrake's theory regard-ing the development of species, but in his insight regarding the physical capacity of bodies to affect one another over intervening space and time. *The lived body is revelatory and effective in ways that exceed our capacity to contain or manipulate.*

In a positive sense, when Francis of Assisi walked through the streets, his body-person, increasingly attuned to Christ, analo-gously became a 'vibrating presence' for those among whom he walked. Those who were 'attuned' began to resonate with that presence: it was a dynamic, personal presence that was *more* than body, but never without the body. When there is integrity of person the 'within' and the 'without' vibrate with the same message; there is a field of 'morphic resonance' into which others can come, be received and respond.

[19] Rupert Sheldrake, *A New Science of Life*, p. 13.
[20] Rupert Sheldrake, *A New Science of Life*, p. 95.

What insights can Sheldrake's hypothesis bring for deepened theological understanding of eucharistic sacramental Presence? for relationships with members of the Communion of Saints? to relics as more than sacred artifacts from the past? Beyond the principles of physics, there is the personal, human capacity to experience a lived-body resonance with Jesus Christ in his resurrected Presence, in whom are assumed all *dabar*-events from the dawn of creation to the present. The Letter to the Colossians employs different terminology but points to the same mystery:

As he is the Beginning,
he was first to be born from the dead,
so that he should be first in every way;
because God wanted all perfection
to be found in him
and all things to be reconciled through him and for him,
everything in heaven and everything on earth,
when he made peace
by his death on the cross (Col. 1:18–20).

After Paul's revelatory encounter with the Risen Christ on the road to Damascus, his life was given to the mystery he had experienced – that of resonating with the Christ-identification within the whole body of believers, and ultimately realizing that 'everything in heaven and everything on earth' is called to be attuned to Christ's redemptive Presence.

When the first disciples responded to John the Baptist's recognition of Jesus as the 'Lamb of God' and followed him along the Jordan, he turned and asked what they sought. Perhaps with some embarrassment over being asked their intent, they asked simply where he lived. His answer also was simple: 'Come and see' (Jn. 1:39). Decades later, the Gospel according to John records with precise intensity: 'so they went and saw where he lived, and stayed with him the rest of that day. It was about the tenth hour' (Jn. 1:39). There are events that indelibly mark personal and universal history, that send vibrations shuddering through the universe. We say of such events: 'It changed the course of history,' or 'The world will never be the same again.' Many years after such turning points, strangers will turn to ask one another, 'Where were you, what were you doing when such-and-such occurred?' The disciples' first visit to Jesus' dwelling place was such an event. Most likely it was an eye-witness, someone who carried the vibrations of that in his body, who could write simply, 'It was about the tenth hour.'

After that introductory meeting Jesus would gradually reveal bodily what it meant for him to be in relation to the Father and the Spirit, and what it meant for the disciples to be in union with him. During the Last Discourse, on the occasion of his total Self-gift in the body and the blood, Jesus revealed at greatest depth the inner identity of God and the possibility of human participation in divine mutual Self-gift. All of creation, on its various levels, is called to participate in this union.[21]

It has been seen that the body is revelatory of the whole person, a Real Symbol. Each human person is a visible, meaningful word spoken bodily into the world, bearing a unique identity. The more that outward expression and inner intent are in accord, the more perfectly is the body-person realized as Real Symbol. It is within this perspective that we will explore the core importance of sexuality within a Theology of the Body.

---

[21] See Sister M. Timothy Prokes, *Mutuality: The Human Image of Trinitarian Love* (Mahwah, NJ, 1993), pp. 16–19.

7

Human Sexuality

FROM the perspective of faith seeking understanding, what does it mean to be a sexual person? Although the human community in general is currently preoccupied with sexual matters, it is necessary to acknowledge from the outset some of the major reasons why there are gaps and inadequacies in commonly held *understandings* of sexuality. Among these are 1) fear; 2) the trivialization of marital covenant; 3) the influence of revisionist theories of morality; 4) the commercialization of sex; and 5) the multiple forms of technical/chemical intervention in human procreation. The last two reasons will be treated at greater length in Chapter Eight, but the first three need to be described briefly here so that there can be greater clarity in arriving at a 'working description' of human sexuality.

First, as we have seen, inadequate understanding regarding sexuality has often resulted in fear, taboo, and continued ignorance. Today one can add the fear of responsibility for new life and fear of sexually transmitted diseases. Two very divergent ways of reacting to fear are 1) instinctual bravado, and 2) integral courage. A passage in Margaret Atwood's novel *Surfacing* illustrates a 'bravado' response to fear. Her protagonist muses on the link between fear and language, noting that there is a distinct difference between the 'French speaking' and the 'English speaking.' She identifies the deepest fears of each linguistic group by noting how these get 'translated' into daily speech. The novel's protagonist maintains that people heap contemptuous words and phrases on the objects of their fear as a way of coping with them and dispelling their power. She muses:

> There are no dirty words any more, they've been neutered, now they're only parts of speech; but I recall the feeling, puzzled, baffled, when I found out some words were dirty and the rest were clean. The bad ones in French are the religious ones, the

worst ones in any language were what they were most afraid of and in English it was the body, that was even scarier than God.[1]

The literary observation about the 'English-speaking' is borne out by graffiti and the communications media's repetitious use of words associated with genital activity and excretion.

It is often asserted that uninhibited sexual behavior and explicit discussion of it are desirable ways of exorcizing fear and overcoming centuries of needless restraint. Many who formerly might have shielded their deviancy or sought professional assistance, now seek public display and affirmation. Atwood's astute perceptions regarding language and fear resonate with Rudolph Otto's description of responses to the 'holy': in each case there is an experience of both fascination and dread. Sexuality participates in the mystery of the human vocation to be image and likeness of God and it is profoundly linked to the 'holy.' For that reason it is filled with tensions that cannot be resolved through bravado or boundless public display. Neither is sexuality to be suppressed as the object of a taboo.

As seen in Chapter One, designating something 'taboo' in earlier times meant the attempt to control or placate powerful and dangerous forces (the truths of their reality often obscured or misunderstood). There are analogies, however, between ritual ways of dealing with taboos and contemporary methods of responding to fertility and sexual behavior. The condom is a primary example, a kind of talisman thought to make its users invincible; similarly, the slogan 'safer sex' has become a kind of secular mantra for preventing AIDS. There are differences, however, between ancient and contemporary perceptions of fertility and sexuality as dangerous. In earlier times, taboo rituals were practiced in order to *enhance* fertility for humans, animals and the earth and to placate fertility goddesses so that they would be favorable. In contradistinction, most contraceptives and surgical interventions are now sought in order to *thwart* fertility. In either case, there is a common fear that fertility requires external intervention. Formerly, rituals and potions were used so that fertility goddesses would assure new life, whereas today many seek professional assistance in order to assure sterility or controlled means of conception/gestation.

[1] Margaret Atwood, *Surfacing* (Toronto, 1972), p. 45.

THE INFLUENCE OF REVISIONIST MORAL THEORIES

There is a second reason for 'gaps and inadequacies' in commonly held understandings of sexuality: revisionist moral theories that interpret it inadequately. In his encyclical *Veritatis Splendor* Pope John Paul II discussed teleological moral theories (there are various forms, some designated 'consequentialist,' some 'proportionalist,' some 'situationist') which 'maintain that it is never possible to formulate an absolute prohibition of particular kinds of behavior which would be in conflict in every circumstance and in every culture'[2] with the values indicated by reason and Revelation. According to teleological theories, the significant aspects to be considered in evaluating the goodness of human acts are 1) the subject's intention; 2) the foreseeable consequences of an act; and 3) the proportion between good and bad effects of that act.[3] From this perspective there are no acts which can be considered *intrinsically* evil. Only after weighing the proportion between the possible good and bad effects of an act can it be determined what should be chosen as a given course of action and what may need to be chosen as the greater good or the lesser evil in a particular situation. Prior to this determination an act remains 'pre-moral' since its moral specificity depends upon the circumstances and a given person's values, charity and prudence. Thus, theorists of this persuasion hold that the judgment and choice of a sincere person may be incompatible with traditional moral precepts. For those who hold a 'proportional' approach to moral decision-making, traditional moral norms (even those concerning serious sexual matters) have a relative quality. They are open to exceptions and must be evaluated in light of circumstances and personal intent.

Subscribing to these moral guidelines trivializes human sexuality, reducing its *meaning* to that assigned to it by particular cultures or individuals. Even for communities of faith, objective moral norms can be superseded by the personal convictions of

---

[2] Pope John Paul II, *Veritatis Splendor*, Vatican trans. in *Origins*, 23, 18, October 14, 1993, p. 320.
[3] See Pope John Paul II, *Veritatis Splendor*, p. 320.

esteemed theologians and/or the results of opinion polls. *If there are no enduring truths of reality concerning sexuality that transcend individual determinations, cultures and historical eras*, any human act can ultimately be rationalized in the name of love and compassion.

This is crucial when seeking faith understanding of sexuality since it concerns 1) the very understanding of what it means to be a sexual person; and 2) the possibility of the Church's speaking with certainty regarding moral decision-making, and the enduring meaning of sexuality in relation to the basic mysteries of faith.

This is exemplified in Charles Curran's essay marking the twenty-fifth anniversary of *Humanae Vitae* in which he described his own efforts to thwart the effectiveness of the encyclical through organized dissent. On the day prior to public release of the encyclical, he gathered a group of theologians to discuss it. They concluded that it 'offered no new arguments' and that it would cause 'great problems for the church.' Reflecting twenty-five years later on the statement of dissent that he had drafted,[4] Curran insisted that the Church had lost its credibility regarding sexuality because of its position on artificial contraception 'and other issues.' The Magisterium, he said, needs to abandon a moral methodology that is permanent and unchanging regarding sexuality and admit that its teaching on contraception is wrong (even though he maintained that contraception has become a 'dead issue'). Implied in Curran's analysis of events since the promulgation of *Humanae Vitae* is the conviction that majority opinion and common praxis are valid measures of moral rectitude regarding sexuality.

It has been important to cite both fear and inadequate moral theories as major difficulties in seeking the theological meaning of human sexuality. They can prevent a probing of the fundamental questions: 1) what does it *mean* to be a sexual person?

---

[4] Curran wrote: 'After much discussion, I drafted a statement that was accepted with some modifications, indicating our evaluation of the encyclical, disagreeing with its specific ethical conclusion about birth control, asserting the common (but not well-known) teaching that Catholics may dissent from authoritative noninfallible church teaching, and concluding that Catholic spouses could responsibly decide in some circumstances to use artificial contraception.' Charles Curran, 'Encyclical Left Church Credibility Stillborn,' *National Catholic Reporter* (July 16, 1993), p. 14.

and 2) does sexuality have a meaning that exceeds the limits of individual cultures, moments of history and subjective choices?

A third 'gap and inadequacy' regarding commonly held understandings of sexuality can be seen in the radical reinterpretation of spousal and familial relationships that has taken place in the West in recent decades. The conclusion of the twentieth century has been marked by a widespread dissolution of monogamous marriages and the family unit centered in mother, father and children. Accompanying this dissolution is the conviction that a variety of sexual lifestyles have equal validity. This dissipates scriptural understandings of sexuality – understandings conveyed in the language of covenant and spousal fidelity. This diminishment of a scriptural basis has repercussions for both covenantal marriage and consecrated celibacy. If commonly held understandings of sexuality are inadequate, how recognize authentic characteristics of sexuality which are crucial for ongoing development of Body Theology? We have already seen that in the human vocation to be image and likeness of God, the body is revelatory, that it is the Real Symbol of the whole person.

WHAT IS HUMAN SEXUALITY?

Let us begin with a 'working definition': sexuality is our human capacity as whole persons to enter into love-giving, life-giving union in and through the body in ways that are appropriate. Each aspect of this description is significant. First of all, our sexuality is totally human. It is not an animalistic drive identical to that found in subhuman species. Human sexuality is *person-al*, involving the giving and receiving of person-gift. Robert Joyce says: 'Sexuality, then, can be defined as the personal power *to share* (physically, psychically, and spiritually) *the gift of self* with self and with others. Sexuality is basically the power of sharing self. Sharing involves giving and receiving – not giving and getting.'[5] Only persons can be sexual in this manner. Further it is a human *capacity*. This means that the ability to share the person-self is not restricted to certain bodily organs and activities, nor is

[5] Robert Joyce, *Human Sexual Ecology: A Philosophy and Ethics of Man and Woman* (Washington, D.C., 1981), p. 19.

95

it confined to a certain portion of life. It is a capacity of the whole person, pervading the entire lifetime. As the two creation accounts of Genesis indicate, to be human is to be constituted a sexual person.

When Pope John Paul II began his series of Audiences on marriage, he followed the example of Jesus Christ and referred to the theological narratives of 'the beginning' in Genesis, basing the meaning of sexuality and marriage in the human vocation that was given in creation. Michel Seguin writes:

> What are we to conclude from this original meaning given by God to sexuality from the beginning of creation, as expressed in these splendidly rich analyses of John Paul II? The first and fundamental statement which summarizes in two words the whole philosophical and theological conception which the pope has of the human person (his anthropology) boils down to the statement that the person is a 'being-gift.'[6]

It is on the foundation of Revelation and body-experience (that is, on the basis of Body Theology) 'that we have come to conclude that in his most profound reality the human person is a "being-gift." '[7] Sexuality is our *capacity* as whole persons to enter into life-giving love union in and through the body. Sexuality enables us bodily to *be* person-gift. This derives from each human person's being created in the image and likeness of God, the Trinity of Persons who are in constant perichoretic union through total Self-gift to the other Persons, and through total receptivity to the Self-gift of the other Persons. It is Jesus' revelation concerning divine inner life that gives a context for understanding human sexuality in its foundational sense as revelatory self-gift. In his final discourse, Jesus brought to supreme Revelation what he had prepared his immediate followers to receive throughout his public life with them. Within prayer at the Last Supper, he spoke of his life of union with the Father and the Spirit in terms of mutual Self-gift, of complete personal giving and receiving. The theology of God's inner life (and thus, of human

[6] Michel Seguin, 'The Biblical Foundations of the Thought of John Paul II on Human Sexuality,' *Communio*, XX, 2 (Summer, 1993), pp. 276–277.
[7] Michel Seguin, 'The Biblical Foundations of the Thought of John Paul II on Human Sexuality,' p. 277.

life in that image) is a 'gift theology,' a faith reflection upon the irrevocable givenness and receptivity among the divine Persons.[8] Faith-based understandings of human sexuality take their starting point in the trinitarian mystery.

It is not only the present age that questions the meaning of sexuality. Nor has it ever been a 'simple' question. When Jesus was asked a specific question regarding divorce, he responded by recalling the original intent of God who created humanity in relationship, male and female (see Matt. 19:1–12). His disciples were bewildered by his insistence on marital fidelity, pointing out that Moses had allowed divorce in specific cases. Transcending their search for a limited answer, Jesus assured them that it was not so 'from the beginning.' Hardness of heart would not excuse the need to receive the meaning of faithful body-gift already expressed in the very act of creation.

Sexuality is an enduring capacity of the whole person. Already in the womb a child experiences the capacity bodily in an elemental but profound manner. At no time in later life will there be the same capacity to *reside* – *to live within another physically* or to share flesh and blood with such enduring immediacy. Womb-life is a prelude to the mature capacity of living within one another in the manner that Christ prayed for in his Last Discourse: 'May they be one in us, as you are in me and I am in you, so that the world may believe it was you who sent me' (Jn. 17:21). Human sexuality expresses the entire person's capacity to be forever-gift – the genesis of every individual child meant to be a creative 'third,' the expression of selves offered totally, and received unreservedly. The *call* to be person-gift is already signed in the moment of conception and it is a capacity that can unfold through life in its various stages.

This means that sexuality is not encapsulated in the reproductive organs nor is it relegated to the period of life between puberty and the diminishment of genital activity. Since we are constituted sexual persons, this capacity is not simply an optional feature of humanness, or a faculty understood only in a genitally-related sense. As *constitutive* of the person, it participates in what Pope John Paul has termed the 'nuptial meaning of the body.' The entire body-person is destined for life-giving, love-

---

[8] See Sister M. Timothy Prokes, *Mutuality*, pp. 15–37.

union in and through the body in ways that are appropriate to one's age, one's state of life and commitment.

Everyone – married couples, those consecrated in celibacy, aged and infirm persons, as well as children – are constituted sexual persons, with the vocation to be bodily love-giving, life-giving in countless ways. When there is a misunderstanding (or a blurring) of the appropriate ways to express this capacity there is a devastation of persons because the sexual capacity touches those incommunicable depths where each person is called into union with God as well as with other human persons. When sexuality is interpreted as the indiscriminate ability to take and be taken, simply for the sake of pleasure or gain, it is the whole person that is violated or made into an object.

'One Flesh'

Within sacramental marriage, there is an exclusive permanent covenant between a man and a woman, their uninhibited mutual self-gift consummated in that intercourse which seals their becoming indissolubly 'one flesh.' It is, as St. Paul says in Ephesians 5, a sacramental witness to the mystery of the union between Christ and the Church. The particular characteristics of married self-gift in and through the body are 1) its permanence; 2) its exclusivity; and 3) its orientation to the conception and nurturing of new personal life. It is only within this understanding of marriage that the multiple questions concerning responsible regulation of conception can be adequately pursued.

In covenantal, sacramental marriage, the spouses become *one flesh*. In the intimate personal acts which express that exclusive, integral union there is no place for barriers, rejection or deceit. Sacramental marriage is simultaneously the outward manifestation of marital covenant and witness to the embodied inviolate union of Christ with the Church. Those entering into marital covenant make a mutual promise of body-fidelity that encompasses all their expressions of love-giving and life-giving. In the previous chapter, the lived body was described as revelatory of the whole person, as Real Symbol, in which outward manifestation is meant to be 'at one' with inner meaning and intent. The revelatory aspect of person is realized profoundly through sexuality since it is precisely the capacity to be given and received in love-giving, life-giving body union. It has been seen that every human 'gesture' (expressive not simply of a part of the body, but the whole person) should be honest, that is 'at-one' with the person's inner intent, and revelatory of inner meaning. Further, it has been seen that genuine, personal self-revelation cannot be forced or earned. It can only be given and received as gift: self-revelation is a making-known that exceeds all calculation. When a person 'lives the body' into an expression of love-giving, life-giving union, the more intimate that expression, the more integral it should be. Edmond Barbotin says:

> ... meaning is 'embodied' in the gesture, in virtue of the essential soul-body union; the meaning is immanent in the bodily signifying.... Our 'complicity' as human beings becomes a kind of empathic grasp of the language of gesture and posture.... At once the current of meaning flows, the spark of understanding is struck, not at the level of abstract knowledge but at the level of lived experience and immediate presence.[9]

If gestures reveal persons, says Barbotin, they do have an objective meaning (or else they would not serve in communicating). There is, in fact, a 'spontaneously recognized meaning' in gestures. That gestures can be falsified 'by a subjective intention which is contrary to the patent meaning confirms the objectivity'[10] of gestures, says Barbotin. The profoundly person-involving 'gesture' of marital intercourse (whether spontaneous or planned) bears a meaning that requires honesty. That is why the teachings of the Catholic Church which address the lived meaning of sexuality are consistent in emphasizing the unity between unitive and procreative aspects of genital intercourse. The teachings are not legal impositions: they are consistent affirmations of what it means to be constituted a sexual person. The context for these teachings is that of person-gift (created in the image of the Trinity). Whatever is purposely done to prevent the full reality of person-gift and full mutual receptivity of the other body-person in the act of intercourse falsifies the 'gesture.' It is for this reason that artificial contraception and deliberate sterilization lack the

---

[9] Edmond Barbotin, *The Humanity of Man*, p. 192.
[10] Edmond Barbotin, *The Humanity of Man*, p. 221.

'truth of the reality' signified in intercourse. Arthur Vogel says in *Body Theology*:

> Meaning is in words as we are in our bodies, and it is only because we are our bodies that we can 'be' our words – or, as it is usually put, mean what we say.... Double-talk is a way in which a person tries to be in two places at the same time – for we can avoid taking a stand verbally as well as physically.[11]

Genesis describes woman and man prior to their sinning as living in 'original nakedness,' without shame. Sin ruptured their inner integrity and this was outwardly manifest in the way that their bodily presence was *lived* in response to God, to one another and to the rest of creation. There was a wounding of person-gift, resulting in blame, dominion, toil, and death. There was a need to shield the body from one another. Conversely, in the act of redemption, Jesus Christ was bodily stripped and revealed in naked, restorative integral gift.

Jesus Brings Sexuality to its Fullest Expression

The 'Paschal Mystery' is one event, beginning with the Last Supper and opening forever into resurrection Presence. At the Last Supper, Jesus brought the capacity of human sexuality to its fullness, sealing forever his total Self-gift in the body and the blood. When his stripped body was raised on the cross, the original nakedness of love-giving, life-giving union in and through the body was restored. He brought the 'nuptial meaning of body' to its fullest expression in an irrevocable manifestation of love.

There are many differing theological opinions among Christians concerning the meaning of sexuality, marriage and family. The consistent magisterial teaching of the Roman Catholic Church is that every spousal act of intercourse, from the 'truth of its reality' just discussed, is to remain open to new life. Some theologians hold that couples who are basically open to new life can occasionally and for 'good reasons' use contraceptives in

---

[11] Arthur Vogel, *Body Theology*, p. 92.

order to avoid the conception of new life. Moral theologian William May dismisses a 'partial' openness to new life. He considers it equivalent to saying: if I am basically honest with you it doesn't matter if now and again I lie to you. In his recent work, *Marriage: The Rock on Which the Family is Built*, May writes:

> If a couple were deliberately to do something to impede the communication of spousal love, they would be acting in a nonmarital way; they would not be open to the gift of marital love. Likewise, if they were deliberately to do something, either prior to their marital embrace, during it, or subsequent to it, precisely to impede the handing on of human life, their union would not be truly marital.[12]

While it is possible to avoid truth-telling in minor matters without devastating results, the more sublime and person-involving the matter requiring truth-telling, the greater the need for integrity. In the case of marital intercourse, *the very persons bonded in one flesh are the matter of communicative exchange requiring truthful self-gift*. If they say bodily, 'I give myself totally to you', while simultaneously subverting that communication, it is not just a question of an isolated imperfect act interspersed in a long sequence of 'faithful' acts. It is the subversion of covenantal fidelity, an untruthfulness acted out bodily, whether or not they have agreed upon it.

In marriage, as in every human relationship, each act that expresses love union in and through the body is intrinsically ordered toward what is appropriate, honest and life-giving. This is freeing rather than inhibiting. The joy, even exuberance of love union, depends ultimately on the freedom of truth and allows uninhibited self-gift. We have seen that to be human is to be constituted a sexual person, created to be love-giving and life-giving in and through the body in ways that are appropriate. That means that *most* personal relationships in life are meant to be celibate (whether one is married or not). In addition to one's spouse, a married woman or man will have multiple relationships. Each of these is a body-relationship, called to be fruitful, life-giving in ways that are appropriate. They are a participation

---

[12] William May, *Marriage: The Rock on Which the Family is Built* (San Francisco, 1995), p. 129.

in Christ's spousal mystery of union with his Body, the Church. To block or destroy the responsibility of new life arising from them is to assume a contraceptive/abortive mentality.

The celibate earthly Jesus lived a constant interchange of love with all who would receive him, laying down his life bodily day after day in ways fitting to the diverse persons, times and places. At one point he described his mission: 'so that they may have life and have it to the full' (Jn. 10:10). Ultimately, he sealed his covenantal redeeming love for all humanity in the perpetual gift of his body and blood. There is a coherence among the mysteries of faith. It is not surprising that rejection of integral sexual activity also involves resistance to the maintaining of enduring moral norms and a questioning of eucharistic Real Presence. To touch one is to touch all. Writing a few years after the promulgation of *Humanae Vitae*, Charles Curran stressed the need for conditioning the teachings of Jesus to meet contemporary 'realities' and the need to compromise. 'The ethic of Jesus might be sublime and beautiful,' he said, 'but the teaching of Jesus seems impossible and irrelevant for the daily life of Christians.'[13] There was need for compromise, he said: 'A true follower of Jesus cannot dismiss his whole ethical teaching as irrelevant and meaningless for daily existence,' but:

> ... I have developed a theory of compromise theology precisely because of the inadequacy of Catholic ethics to come to grips with sin-filled situations. Sometimes the presence of sin in the world will force one to do something which, if there were no sin present, should not be done.[14]

Once one holds that the sin condition of the world *forces* us to do something that should not be done, there are no genuine moral boundaries. If it is believed that the human person is incapable of avoiding certain sinful actions, there is a simultaneous readiness to look for assistance from forces external to the human person. Technology and medicine, for example, can then be used in ways that replace authentic human sexual expression.

[13] Charles Curran, *Themes in Fundamental Moral Theology* (Notre Dame, IN, 1974), p. 11.
[14] Charles Curran, *New Perspectives in Moral Theology* (Notre Dame, IN, 1974), p. 75. See also Charles E. Curran, *A New Look at Christian Morality* (Notre Dame, IN, 1968), pp. 171–173.

When do such interventions *assist* in that genuine expression and when do they cross the horizon of therapeutic assistance and diminish the capacity to be an authentically human sexual person? It will be necessary to explore this in the following chapter.

8

Technology and the Lived Body

IN the latter part of the twentieth century, technological and medical interventions offer the potential for remaking humanity, for the most part in a secularized society that does not refer to a divine Creator or the affirmation of Ephesians 3:10–11: 'How comprehensive God's wisdom really is, exactly according to the plan which he had had from all eternity in Christ Jesus our Lord.' Examples from the popular media illustrate a variety of moral/anthropological problems that accompany biological and medical advances in a rapidly developing technological society that lacks cohesive agreement on the meaning of the lived body and the human vocation within creation.

The Reuter News Service of London, for example, has reported three technological forays into the conception of human life:

1 Following artificial insemination at a Rome clinic, a fifty-nine-year-old woman in Britain carried and gave birth to twins.

2 An 'egg' (presumably fertilized, and hence, a newly-conceived child) from a white woman was implanted in the womb of a black woman, whose husband of mixed race wanted to 'ensure' the child's color.

3 British doctors revealed an unprecedented development in genetic engineering which they described as a 'fertility treatment.' It involved taking eggs from the ovaries of aborted female fetuses, fertilizing them with sperm, and then implanting them into a woman's womb. It is projected that the first baby 'created from a dead fetus' could be born within three years. The doctors who developed this process consider it a solution to what they term a 'serious shortage of donor eggs' from ethnic minorities.

A British legislator, Dame Jill Knight, expressed alarm at the use of ova from aborted fetuses, saying: 'I do not understand how the medical profession could consider producing children from a mother that never existed.'[1] She pondered what effect this would have on a child who eventually 'realizes the basic truth.'

THE BODY AS ARTIFACT

Cosmetic surgery is used extensively to refashion the lived body. (The Academy of Cosmetic Surgery reported that a half million cosmetic surgeries had been performed in the United States in 1992.) Parents have used various types of cosmetic surgery as gifts for their children at Christmas or when they 'come of age.' There is also what is called 'art by personal body transformation,' exemplified by French performance artist 'Orlan':

> According to the magazine Art in America, she is having parts of her face and body modified to conform to Renaissance and post-Renaissance ideals of feminine beauty, and when she finishes, an advertising agency will select a name for her reflecting her new persona.[2]

Exploitation of the human body as an 'art form' or 'protest form' extends to the dead. Paula Span, reflecting on memorial services held for performance artists who have died from AIDS, has said that the most moving music and dance in New York occurs in theatrical performances for which no tickets are sold. They occur as memorial performances or political statements, sometimes the corpse itself becoming the statement. Artist David Wojnarowicz had imagined that the bodies of those who had died from AIDS would be taken to Washington, D.C. and deposited on the White House steps. After his death, this was realized analogously.[3] Many no longer find meaning in rituals which relate suffering, dying and death to a transcendent personal God.

[1] Cited in 'Dander's Up Over "Designer Babies",' in *Calgary Herald* (January 2, 1994), p. A2.
[2] 'One Artist's Body of Work,' *The Washington Post* (December 26, 1993), p. C3.
[3] See Paula Span, 'Dying Is an Art,' *The Washington Post* (January 2, 1994), p. G6. The body of Mark Fisher, in fulfillment of a desire expressed before his death, was taken to Bush-Quayle campaign headquarters on the eve of the presidential election and a person with AIDS, using a bullhorn, charged Bush with Fisher's 'murder.'

Accordingly, bodies of the deceased, rather than being venerated as relics, are objectivized or 'used' instrumentally.

Numerous questions about the interrelationship between the body-person and the 'work of our hands' emerge from the examples just cited. The technological, medical and mechanical tools which humans have fashioned are now used, in turn, to refashion their makers. For that reason, it must be clarified that laboratories of the life-sciences and the brilliant technical inventions of this age do not supersede the human persons who fashioned them, nor do they have a separate existence from those given responsibility for stewardship of the earth.

Early in the 1960s it became evident that the refashioning of the human body-person would be the most consequential effort of humanity as it moved into the twenty-first century. During the first generation after World War Two, the world community expressed horror over atrocities committed under Nazism. The calculated disposal of an entire people was partially realized in order that a 'master race' might rule the earth. Grim documentation details some of the ruthless experiments conducted upon victims in concentration camps. Gradually, however, horror was dulled by familiarity, which at times turned to fascination and imitation. Even the most violent and bizarre acts can become so familiar *that they begin to seem reasonable, defensible – at times desirable – as solutions to immediate problems*. The unthinkable becomes 'thinkable.' Recently, new questions have been posed: should we begin to examine the results of Nazi experiments in order to utilize their findings? Does the fact that these findings were obtained in evil ways mean that they should not be applied?

HOW THE UNTHINKABLE BECOMES THINKABLE, DESIRABLE

Three disparate developments in recent decades have abetted the tendency to accept as reasonable what formerly seemed reprehensible: 1) there was the loss (philosophical, theological, and scientific/technological) of a common understanding of what it means to be a human person; 2) there was an erosion of a common moral sense; and 3) the popular media have abetted the manipulation of body-persons through whetting a common appetite for the bizarre and sensational.

At a national conference on the teaching of medical ethics in 1972, Joseph Fletcher began to designate a profile of character-istics for determining 'humanness.' He listed what he termed fifteen positive and five negative criteria for determining who ought to be included in the category 'human.' Among his criteria were these: a) before achieving minimal intelligence or after its irretrievable loss, there is no personal status (Fletcher went so far as to say that anyone scoring less than forty in a Standard Stanford-Binet IQ Test is 'questionably' a person, and anyone scoring less than twenty is not a person); b) of any individual not self-controllable he said, 'a low level of life is reached about on a par with a paramecium'; and c) 'man' is not non-artificial, so a baby artificially produced through 'deliberate and careful con-trivance, would be more *human* than one resulting from sexual roulette, the reproductive mode of the subhuman species.'[4]

A second development, closely linked to the above, and dis-cussed briefly in the previous chapter, is the erosion of a common moral sense that formerly provided a framework for human interaction. Once there is a denial of enduring norms that safe-guard the inviolable dignity and worth of every human person, it can seem reasonable to eliminate from the human family those who are considered unfit or defective. Along with the dismissal of some is the attempt to attain ever more perfected models of humanity.

Third, the public media abet the manipulation of the lived body by providing programs and reports which feature the devi-ant and the sensational, so that sensibility is dulled and what was formerly thought 'unthinkable' can seem commonplace.

On the one hand, daily technological advances and the rapid-ity of communication provide the possibility of enhancing human life in its uniqueness, allowing stewardship of the earth to advance. On the other hand, there is the possibility that the body-person might be altered so radically that there would be a sever-ance between the contrived 'human being' and body-persons

---

[4] See Joseph Fletcher, 'Indicators of Humanhood: A Tentative Profile of Man,' *The Hastings Center Report*, 2, 5 (November, 1972), pp. 1–4.

intimately related to divine creation, Revelation and redemptive Incarnation. Robert Brungs, speaking of applying the methods of physics to the life sciences, has noted that 'Scientists will try to describe the human physical composition in a series of equations, thus creating a generic model of the human being from a physical-chemical point of view.'[5] Care must be taken, he said, not to equate these descriptions of purely physical processes with the identity of what it means to be a human being.

There are fundamental principles which provide a basis for discerning which technical/scientific applications are therapeutic and health-enhancing opportunities and which procedures violate persons or are directed toward the radical alteration of the human being. Three significant documents have provided such basic principles regarding medical/technical issues as these relate to human embodiment: *Humanae Vitae* (Of Human Life); *Donum Vitae* (The Gift of Life); and *Veritatis Splendor* (The Splendor of Truth).[6] It is impossible to synthesize each of these documents in a book which simply lays groundwork for a Theology of the Body. It is possible here only to point out basic insights contained in each of the three documents, showing how each coinheres in the others and provides principles for dealing with practical issues.

HUMANAE VITAE

Promulgated in 1968, *Humanae Vitae* proved to be a watershed document. Pope Paul VI opened his encyclical with a recognition of new questions concerning the regulation of human births. He cited concerns regarding 1) overpopulation; 2) the tendency of governments to take radical measures to curtail population growth; 3) the changing nature of work, living conditions, education and economics; 4) the impact of new understandings concerning women; 6) a deepened appreciation for conjugal love in marriage; and 7) the 'stupendous' development of the human capacity to dominate all aspects of life, particularly those con-

---

[5] Robert Brungs, *You See Lights Breaking Upon Us*, p. 25.
[6] The *Catechism of the Catholic Church* also articulates a comprehensive, integrated understanding of the human person within which to deal with specific issues.

cerning the transmission of life. In light of these issues, Paul VI articulated urgent questions of the time: would it be better to revise ethical norms that required sacrifices – even heroic sacrifices at times? By extending the 'principle of totality,' could it be that a couple's responsibility for procreation could be seen in the *ensemble* of their conjugal acts, not simply in their individual acts?

These matters had already concerned his predecessor, Pope John XXIII, who in 1963 established a commission to study them. Paul VI enlarged this commission of world experts so that they might advise him regarding the complex matters surrounding marriage, fertility and responsible parenthood. Within the encyclical he expressed gratitude for the work of the Commission, but stated that their conclusions could not dispense him from personal examination of the issues. He concluded that the Commission's majority report contained proposals which departed from the Catholic Church's consistent moral teaching on marriage. After careful study and prayer on the documentation provided by majority and minority reports, Paul VI issued *Humanae Vitae*, giving his reply to grave questions regarding responsible regulation of human births. The 'problem' of birth, he said, had to be considered beyond any partial perspective: 'in the light of an integral vision of man and of his vocation, not only his natural and earthly, but also his supernatural and eternal vocation.'[7]

It was on this basis that he provided a synthesis of principles underlying responsible regulation of births. Marriage is not a product of chance or evolution, but is humanity's primary way of sacramentalizing the Creator's design of love. Through their reciprocal, personal and exclusive self-gift, husband and wife tend toward a communion of being, not only to realize their mutual perfection, but also to collaborate with God in bringing to life and educating their children. Marital love is fully human, a special form of friendship in which everything is shared without calculating individual gain. The marriage of woman and man is a *covenant* of love, faithful and exclusive, that images the union of Christ with the Church (see #8–9). Responsible parenthood

---

[7] Pope Paul VI, *On the Regulation of Birth: Humanae Vitae* (Washington, D.C., 1968), #7, p. 4. Subsequent citations are from this publication.

requires a clarity concerning the life-giving laws inherent in persons, and includes the need for control of instinct and passion. Since responsible decision-making regarding the conception of children requires a 'profound relationship to the objective moral order established by God' (#10), spouses, in transmitting life, 'are not free to proceed completely at will, as if they could determine in a wholly autonomous way the honest path to follow ...' (#10). The creative intent of God is expressed in the very nature of marriage, in its natural laws and patterns of fertility, which, if known and respected, *provide for normal periods of infecundity*. It is the constant teaching of the Church, said Paul VI, that every marriage act 'must remain open to the transmission of life' (#11). This is not an arbitrary human norm; since there is a God-willed inseparable connection between the unitive and procreative meanings of each conjugal act:

> To use this divine gift destroying, even if only partially, its meaning and its purpose is to contradict the nature both of man and of woman and of their most intimate relationship, and therefore it is to contradict also the plan of God and His Will (#13).

Because of the intrinsic unity of love-giving and life-giving in human intercourse – blocking, interrupting or chemically negating the act is inherently wrong and ultimately devastating to both persons. If intercourse is lived out in this fashion, the body is made to express only a *simulation* of total self-gift. The entire body-self acts dishonestly in a matter of utmost seriousness at the heart of covenantal relationship and is violated at the depths of Real Symbol. It is the truth of reality and not an abstract legal requirement that reveals to woman and man the depth meaning of this act. The encyclical takes cognizance of human weakness and vulnerability. Spouses need encouragement in remaining faithful to the enduring meaning of intercourse:

> ... so that they must not be offered some easy means of eluding its observance. It is also to be feared that the man, growing used to the employment of anti-conceptive practices, may finally lose respect for the woman and, no longer caring for her physical and psychological equilibrium, may come to the point of considering her as a mere instrument of selfish enjoyment, and no longer as his respected and beloved companion (#17).

While this teaching makes the Church a sign of contradiction, said Paul VI, it can never declare licit what unchangeably opposes the true good of the person. There are unsurmountable limits to the possibilities of human dominion over the body and its functions – limits which no individual or human authority can surpass without harm. As seen above, protests accompanied the promulgation of *Humanae Vitae* and the struggle continues over principles enunciated in it, although many have simply dismissed these principles as irrelevant in the realm of personal choice.

DONUM VITAE

Donum Vitae, familiarly known as an 'Instruction on Respect for Human Life in Its Origin and on the Dignity of Procreation,'[8] builds upon anthropological and moral principles enunciated in previous magisterial teaching: those which uphold the dignity of the human person as endowed with a spiritual soul and destined for 'beatific communion with God,' (p. 6) and having the right to life and respect. The document states that while the Magisterium does not claim specific competence in the experimental sciences, it has an apostolic duty and mission to respond to the data of research and technology. It would be an illusion, the document states, to think that scientific research and its applications are morally neutral or that moral decisions can be grounded in technical efficiency and usefulness. The body-person is unified, so that the body cannot be treated as a 'mere complex of tissues, organs and functions, nor can it be evaluated in the same way as the body of animals; rather it is a constitutive part of the person who manifests and expresses himself through it' (p. 8). Doctors and biologists enjoy scientific competence but it is not within their province to determine human origins and destinies.

In responsible collaboration with God's fruitful love, 'the gift of human life must be actualized in marriage through the specific and exclusive acts of husband and wife, in accordance with the laws inscribed in their persons and in their union' (p. 11). Once

[8] Congregation for the Doctrine of the Faith, *Instruction on Respect for Human Life in its Origin and on the Dignity of Procreation: Replies to Certain Questions of the Day*, Vatican trans. (Boston, MA, issued February 22, 1987). Subsequent page citations are from this publication of the text.

this principle is acknowledged, multiple questions regarding technical interventions can be resolved competently. For example, prenatal diagnoses and therapeutic procedures are desirable which respect the life and integrity of the embryo/fetus and have the purpose of healing or safeguarding the vulnerable unborn child. Any experimental procedures carried out on embryos (whether they are viable or not) are illicit if they are not directly therapeutic for the child (see p. 17).

Donum Vitae reiterates the consistent teaching of the Roman Catholic Church that the unity of marriage requires a wife and husband to become parents only through each other. Every child has the right to be conceived, carried in the womb, and nurtured in growth within a faithful marriage. Every person, however, has inestimable worth, *regardless of the indignities and abuse surrounding its conception and vulnerable prenatal life.* Embryos, living or dead, are to be respected in the same manner as any other human person. They are not objects which can be manipulated, cryopreserved, experimented upon, or disposed of as commercial products or waste (see pp. 15–19). Moreover:

> Certain attempts to influence chromosomic or genetic inheritance are not therapeutic but are aimed at producing human beings selected according to sex or other predetermined qualities. These manipulations are contrary to the personal dignity of the human being and his or her integrity and identity (p. 20).

Artificial fertilization (whether the gametes are provided by husband and wife, or by one or more 'donors') betrays the dignity of the couple, the truth of their marriage, and the rights of children. Principles previously articulated in *Humanae Vitae* increase in significance as the forms of artificial conception of children increase. Once the integrity of unitive/procreative meanings of intercourse are dissipated, the varied technical manipulations of human conception become increasingly diverse and bizarre, as evidenced in the initial paragraphs of this chapter.

It is now possible for a child to have five or more 'parents' when 1) the gametes for a child's conception are obtained from disparate 'owners'; 2) the child is then carried in a surrogate mother's womb; and 3) the rearing of the child is provided by one or more women or men.

Until recently the term 'designer children' was used in a scientific-fictional sense. Today it is common coinage in the public media as varied forms of conception become available. Children conceived as *products* of human contriving are also subject to the life-and-death decisions of those who control their early existence. Those in the Petri dish who seem weak or disadvantaged in some way are not implanted in the wombs of prospective mothers. Many have been flushed down laboratory sinks; others have been experimented upon, or sold for commercial uses.

Prior to the mixing of sperm and eggs under clinical conditions, there is the possibility of selecting 'desirable' frozen sperm, considered most apt for producing superior children. 'Donor attributes' are described (seemingly with anonymity) for investors who select the male germ cells they wish to have used in conceiving their child (ova cannot be frozen and survive). In addition to making economic transactions, clinicians and prospective parents may sign agreements which assure that children who are perceived during their womb life to be defective in some way may be aborted, obviating legal responsibility on the part of clinicians and burden on the part of those negotiating for a healthy child. In the literature explaining these procedures, the specific manipulation of conception and early life is often characterized in terms of compassion for married couples or individuals who otherwise could not 'have' a child. In reality, use of such techniques denigrates the meaning of sexuality and fertility. They treat children as commercial products.

VERITATIS SPLENDOR

The encyclical *Veritatis Splendor* clarifies basic principles of morality and succinctly explains the inadequacy of recent moral theories which dissent from them. As a comprehensive expression of moral teaching, *Veritatis Splendor* (meaning The Splendor of Truth) extends far beyond the two documents just cited but it treats in a fresh manner the relationship between embodiment and technology. Pope John Paul II notes that objections to traditional moral teaching now reach beyond limited or occasional dissent. Instead, there is 'an overall and systematic calling into question of traditional moral doctrine on the basis of certain anthropological and ethical presuppositions.'[9] Many consider the Church to be incapable of intervening in moral matters. Some consider her moral teachings as 'unacceptable' unless they remain on the level of mere exhortation, or the proposing of 'values' (see #4).

John Paul II states that the individual subjective conscience cannot by-pass what has been specified in the ten commandments and what corresponds to the law 'written in the heart.' While an individual's conscience allows him/her to hear the call to do good and avoid evil, it does not *create* the good, nor is it an isolated subjective force. *A right conscience must be formed in relation to truth.* It is difficult to affirm that truth exceeds the limits of individual perception when a culture glorifies individual choice as an ultimate value. This is particularly true when individuals judge that technical interventions offer the promise of solving difficult problems:

> The development of science and technology, this splendid testimony of the human capacity for understanding and for perseverance, does not free humanity from the obligation to ask the ultimate religious questions. Rather, it spurs us on to face the most painful and decisive of struggles, those of the heart and of the moral conscience (#1).

The use of scientific discoveries and their technological application to human life is to be determined in light of the integral meaning, dignity and destiny of each human being. Here it is helpful to apply to the uses of technology what has been discussed earlier regarding inadequate teleological moral theories. *Veritatis Splendor* affirms that the most essential element in any human act is its 'object' (i.e. a freely chosen kind of behavior). Currently, the crux of moral argument turns precisely on this point. Proponents of teleological moral theories (i.e. consequentialism, proportionalism, circumstantialist ethics) deny that any 'object' of a human act can be intrinsically evil. While Revelation proposes moral values, they say, it is impossible to formulate absolute prohibitions against certain kinds of behaviors which

---

[9] Pope John Paul II, *Veritatis Splendor*, Vatican trans. *Origins*, 23, 18 (October 14, 1993), #4. Subsequent citations are from this publication of the text.

will apply in every case in every culture. John Paul II, on the other hand, states:

> If acts are intrinsically evil, a good intention or particular circumstances can diminish their evil, but they cannot remove it. They remain 'irremediably' evil acts; per se and in themselves they are not capable of being ordered to God and to the good of the person (#81).

The 'object' of a human act that is intrinsically evil can never be transformed into a 'right' act by good intentions or the desire to adjust to difficult circumstances. It is erroneous, says John Paul II, to hold that it is impossible to qualify certain acts as evil apart from the intention of the agent or the foreseeable consequences that will result for all concerned. To do so would nullify the objective moral order, result in harm to human relationships, ecclesial communion, and 'the truth about the good' (see #82).

It is in this light that the gifts of scientific discovery and technology are to be utilized and their limitations respected. Many interventions now available (or proposed for future development) in the areas of human procreation, medical treatment and the alleviation of pain and suffering can be morally evaluated without great difficulty by persons of good will when the principles just discussed are applied. These principles clarify *why* some actions which are proposed as solutions to difficult problems cannot be ordered to God and the good of the integral human person. Among these are artificial prevention of human conception; laboratory/clinical conception of human life; experimentation on children in the womb; the elimination of new lives which are considered undesirable or defective; and the fashioning of 'designer babies.' These are violations of the human person.

Once it is understood that the body-person is inviolable from the inception of life to the moment of death, it is possible to recognize that certain acts are intrinsically wrong, *regardless of legal judgments, acts of legislatures, or decisions promulgated by the fiat of national or international civil authorities.* Even as abortion, assisted suicide and the sale of fetal tissue are debated within governmental systems, those who recognize such acts as intrinsically wrong will not be overwhelmed by moral uncertainties concerning these activities. The 'splendor of truth' concerning each person's worth, dignity and destiny will reveal why these acts cannot be offered in praise of God or in honest care of human beings. In life and in death the body requires reverence. When it was reported, for example, that corpses were being used in crash tests of motor vehicles, there was no quandary about the moral issue involved. This action was not 'pre-moral' or amoral in light of the experimenters' intentions or the precise circumstances of the tests. It was wrong because it was a violation of the deceased persons' bodies.

Almost daily we hear of striking new possibilities for treating illnesses, for initiating and reshaping human life, and for disposing of unwanted life. These possibilities show the urgency of knowing the principles which underlie reverence for the body-person. Once the latter have been internalized, they allow truthfulness in weighing questions which cannot be resolved superficially. Some issues are extremely complex and careful discernment is needed in applying the principles of respect for human life to discreet cases. The Human Genome Project, for example, a marvel of research, is yielding immense amounts of valuable information. At the same time it raises serious questions regarding its application. The principles enunciated above are helpful in resolving many of these applications; some cases require careful ongoing discernment in order that 'the truth of reality' may be perceived and respected.

As specialized areas of research continue to develop and yield new possibilities for experimental application, it is apparent that moral consultants will need specific expertise in both scientific knowledge and understanding of the lived body in its call to be image and likeness of God. Brain research, allied with surgical techniques and forms of preservation, serves as an apt example here. Already in 1986, Dr. Robert White, neurosurgeon and researcher, reported at a meeting of the Institute for Theological Encounter with Science and Technology that for some years it had been possible at the primate level to transplant both brain and head (which in the laboratory are termed 'preparations') to another body. What can these 'preparations' do? he asked. Does the brain change in these experiments? The researchers do not know yet. What is now done on the level of primate and rat life has immense ramifications for future human experiments. Dr.

White noted how numerous organs or parts of the body have already been transplanted from one person to another:

> If we do heart transplants, heart/lung transplants, and all these other transplants, who does the person become, particularly if we insist on the totality of the body in that individual? It seems to me that we must use the concept of the brain as being in itself the uniqueness of that human individual.[10]

The uniqueness of the human person, as seen earlier, cannot be reduced to the brain nor to any discrete organ or power of the lived body. White's comments underscore the gravity of need for being acquainted with principles cited in this chapter and the need for those involved in various theological pursuits to be in dialogue with researchers and technicians lest the integrity of the living body-person be violated in the probative tasks of research. Technological advances can subdivide the work of human hands – but they can also divide the *worker*, a factor which must now be explored within a faith understanding of the lived body and the universe into which it extends.

[10] Robert White, in dialogue at Institute for Theological Encounter with Science and Technology Workshop: 'Brain Research and Human Consciousness,' Fordyce House, St. Louis, MO, March 15, 1986. See *Proceedings*, p. 87.

9

Bodily 'Working Out Our Salvation'

WORK is one of the characteristics that distinguishes men and women from the rest of created beings. In his encyclical 'On Human Work,' Pope John Paul II notes very deliberately that work, whether manual or intellectual, is a *human activity*. It is 'the mark of a person operating within a community of persons,'[1] and is a fundamental dimension of human earthly existence. In Genesis the original woman and man received the commission: 'Be fruitful, multiply, fill the earth and conquer it' (Gen. 1:28). While the ancient text does not explicitly speak of 'work,' says John Paul, beyond doubt it indirectly indicates a human activity to be carried out in the world. 'Man is the image of God partly through the mandate received from his Creator to subdue, to dominate, the earth. In carrying out this mandate ... every human being, reflects the very action of the Creator of the universe' (#4).

Work is simultaneously our participation in the ongoing co-creation of the universe and a literal 'working out of our salvation' in space and time. It is essential from the outset to reiterate that in the astonishing array of activities among creatures, *work* is a distinctly human activity. Animals do not 'work' – not the wily beasts who cunningly stalk their prey over a period of days nor the domesticated animals who carry burdens or undergo disciplined training for the economic gain of their owners. The Australian sheep dog that separates and herds large flocks for a sheep rancher carries out an impressive feat, but it does not 'work.' Human work is a participation in the 'work' of the Creator and as such is basically personal and relational. Remaining part of the universe, the human person knows and responds

[1] Pope John Paul II, *On Human Work: Laborem Exercens*, Vatican trans. (Boston, MA, issued on September 14, 1981), p. 5. Subsequent citations are from this publication of the text.

to it, and experiences a responsibility for bringing it to its fullest potential.

It is crucial to distinguish human work from animal behavior since many in the Western nations no longer hold a common understanding of the uniqueness of human life/activity. For example, in 'How Man Began,' a *Time* reporter asserted without qualification: 'No single, essential difference separates human beings from other animals – but that hasn't stopped the phrase-makers from trying to find one.'[2] Some today treat animals as equals (or, at times, prefer them to humans), so it is essential to reiterate the clear distinction between human and animal life in developing the meaning of work within a Theology of the Body. Created in the image of God, human persons gifted with intelligence and free will are invited into an eternal relationship with the divine Persons of the Trinity and entrusted with a care of the universe that is expressed through 'work.' Humanity bears responsibility for appropriate care of animal life while maintaining distinctness from it.

The word *work* encompasses a vast range of human activities. For some, it is centered on a few square meters or kilometers of the universe, where energy is daily poured out at a kitchen counter, a computer keyboard, or a rice paddy. For others, work unfolds during transcontinental flights or while making extended forays into outer space. In any case, work is the participation of the entire body-person in the universal mandate to care for the earth in all of its extensions, to order all things toward the triune God in praise and love so that creation may be brought to its fullest realization.

To work is a privilege and to be deprived of meaningful work is dehumanizing. Genesis describes the creation of the universe as a personal divine work. There is an ethical value to human work because it images God's creative activity and because it is carried out by a person (see *On Human Work*, #6). The most eloquent 'gospel of work' is the example of Jesus Christ who was identified as 'the carpenter's son,' and who chose his apostles from those who knew the particulars of physical work in rural areas of Galilee. In Jesus' example one discerns three dimensions of

---

[2] Michael D. Lemonick, 'How Man Began,' *Time*, 143, 11 (March 14, 1994), p. 80.

human work enumerated by John Paul II: 1) human work is personal; 2) it constitutes a foundation for the formation of family life; and 3) it concerns the entire world community in which each person while belonging to a particular culture is simultaneously linked with the vast historical-social incarnations of 'work' in all generations (see #10).

Following the discovery of an ice-mummified body in the Austrian Alps, an archeologist expressed fascination with evidence that the wanderer of approximately 5,300 years ago 'was snatched from life completely outfitted with the implements of everyday existence.'[3] Researchers have been stunned by the sophistication of the iceman's arrows and clothing. Although crude attempts to remove the body from glacial ice destroyed portions of the corpse, clothing and equipment, there is awe among those who study and restore them. The iceman had carried a bow of yew – the finest wood known for that purpose, and not readily available in the Alps. His quiver held a variety of materials useful in preparing bowstring and arrows of an effective design. A U-shaped frame apparently had served as a carrying pack for an assortment of other instruments: a small wooden-handled dagger, a chopping tool, a grass net, a pencil-size stone tool, and birchbark canisters. From the work tools of one man, deep insight has been opened into the world of 3,300 BC.

The iceman had no way of knowing how his body and workmanship would impact on others thousands of years after his death. Imagine his astonishment had someone told him that his feathered arrows, carved from dogwood, would be of immense significance millennia later! The discovery of his preserved body and its outer accoutrements underscores a still deeper truth of reality: the simplest actions of daily life have enduring meaning. This is particularly true of the internal activities that impel them. For example, every human *thought* creates 'waves' that will continue to reverberate through the universe for all time. The nature and quality of each person's work, whether internal or external, takes on significant meaning, either by contributing responsibly to the unfolding of the universe according to the 'truths of reality,' or wounding what has been entrusted in stewardship.

[3] Leon Jaroff, 'Iceman,' *Time*, 140, 17 (October 26, 1992), p. 48.

We *become* what we do. As Teilhard de Chardin said, the lived body is part of the universe that we possess partially, but not totally. To work is to touch the whole of the universe in and through the body. Anyone who collaborates in the Christly mission 'that they might have life and have it to the full' (Jn. 10:10) not only carries out the mandate revealed in Genesis – he/she takes up the fulfillment of a personal vocation. This can be experienced with perceptible immediacy by those who bear and educate children, those who plant and harvest, create communications networks, or fashion beautiful creations in word, sound and motion.

Likewise, engaging in activities that inhibit or destroy the coming-to-be of creation leave a lasting impact upon every other person and upon the universe as a whole. Using one's expertise to abort, euthanize, or concoct commercial products that poison the earth's common resources subverts the human vocation to work for the dynamic fulfillment of creation.

For an understanding of work consonant with a contemporary Theology of the Body, several aspects need to be considered: 1) the radical shift in the nature of work in the twentieth century; 2) the increased difficulty of maintaining integrity in the performance of work; 3) the need for balance between activity and receptivity; 4) justice in all phases of work; and 5) the centrality of self-gift as the ultimate meaning of human work.

The Radical Shift in 'What it Means to Work'

It must be reiterated: only persons *work*. Animals respond to instinct and repetition. Machines and technological creations (as sophisticated as these may be) are the *result* of human work; they are tools that extend the lived body in space and time. The human person is the only earthly creature that the Trinity has created for intimate personal communion with divine Persons. The human worker is a subject, not an instrument to be used as a means of accomplishing some other purpose. In the doing of work, each person is called to enter into ever deeper personal communion.

These principles concerning the *meaning* of work are crucial at a liminal time in history when there is a drastic reordering of work. As recently as the early third of the twentieth century, the majority of the human community was engaged in agriculturally-based pursuits, By the century's end a dramatic shift has occurred. Especially in the so-called developed nations of the West there have been leaps through and beyond the mechanical age and the technological age to the communications age. Muscular tasks of breaking and seeding the earth's surface have significantly diminished. While the construction of asphalt highways continues, it is the creation of ever more complex communications highways that engages increasing numbers of workers. The tools of those confined to keyboards, desks and cubicles are extensions of mind, eye and touch. Information racing through microchips or scudding through space to bounce off satellites at the speed of light has become a major world commodity. Processing it has become a foremost form of work. With it comes the potential to refashion not only the outer universe but the workers themselves.

Significant separations are occurring in this work of processing information. While the Industrial Revolution certainly divided workers from their homes and extended families, today's technologically-paced workplaces intensify separation in new ways. Many commuters hurtle to work across sterile ribbons of pocked concrete, or burrow through the bowels of major cities in isolated capsules, wary of silent co-travelers whose bodies are immediately 'there,' but non-relational. Now the separation from home and family extends to separation from beauty, from the pulse and feel of the earth. Workers who insert microchips into miniature computers or monitor the swirl of canisters on an assembly line have minimal bonding with 'the work of their hands.' To cite these separative factors does not constitute a jeremiad nor does it signal a romantic return to 'peasant' life. It is simply a conscious acknowledgment of facts that signal the changed meaning of work and the challenges that this involves.

When dehumanizing conditions *pervade* work and workplace, dissociations multiply. Many experience work as something from which to escape; they long to be finished with required tasks in order to experience 'real life.' Days away from the job become oases in the desert of labor. Then, that which ought to be the 'mark of a person operating within a community of persons' is lost as a vital, salvific factor of human fulfillment.

In the early 1970s Marshal McLuhan observed how telecommunications media separated body from message, sender from receiver, scenario from reality. Messages projected into space become disembodied, he said, enabling the sender to remain aloof, to lose a sense of responsibility for that which is transmitted to distant receivers. By the 1990s his observation had been concretely realized. The media can be adroitly manipulated to create predetermined impressions. Video segments can give the *appearance* of a real state of affairs, but have little to do with the integral truth of a person or situation. Images can be spliced, interpolated or phased out. A photograph can no longer be considered credible evidence since it is impossible at times to determine whether or not technicians have altered what is purported to be a 'real' occurrence.[4]

'Virtual reality' is a vehicle for creating imaginative scenarios. It only *simulates* reality, but can suggest a 'virtual' interaction with that which is only 'virtually real.' There can be a loss of distinction between reality and what is merely a projection of the seemingly real.

Separation between the person who works and the work of one's hands becomes acute when creative energies are directed toward refashioning workers themselves according to the image and likeness of patterns prepared by technicians. If the human body is perceived as exciting raw data to be shaped according to selective criteria, human work can be separated from the Trinity, the larger human family, and from the revealed meaning of human existence on earth.

The incalculable gifts of scientific and technological expertise require carefully discerned application to human life. The Genome Project again serves as apt example. Already it promises great potential for therapeutic relief and/or prevention of diseases. On the other hand, it opens possibilities for the creation of 'model' human beings from whom all undesirable traits have been eliminated. Robert Brungs has written of the Genome Project:

[4] See Kathy Sawyer, 'Is It Real Or Is It ...?' *The Washington Post* (February 21, 1994), p. A3. Jean Baudrillard calls the present time the Age of Absolute Simulation, and Margaret Crawford (chair of history and theory at Southern California Institute of Architecture in Los Angeles) thinks that 'theming' is the most notable trend in architecture today. 'The fake is replacing the real everywhere', says Crawford: 'the artificial environment is ubiquitous because everyone knows the fake is better than the real.' William Booth, 'Triumph of the Fake,' *The Washington Post* (April 14, 1996), pp. A1, A20.

What does this work (and its results) mean to individuals, to society, to religion in general, and, specifically, Christianity? For me, that is the most significant issue of all. Some molecular biologists are talking about directing our evolution, about creating a 'new human.' While this remains a gleam in the eye of some biologists, it should alert Christians. How, for example, will this scientific 'new human' relate to the 'new human' St. Paul writes about? It is hardly too soon to begin to ponder that relationship.[5]

In retrospect, it can be seen how the narratives of the Old Testament, which describe the sins and failings of ancient ancestors, have a particular cogency at the end of the second millennium of Christian faith understanding. The rainbow stretched before Noah as a sign that utter destruction of humanity would never again emanate from God. This image gave way in the twentieth century to the mushroom cloud, signaling human openness to nuclear destruction *because it was possible.* Parker Palmer has reflected upon a television documentary called 'The Day After Trinity.' 'Trinity,' he notes, was the ironic code-name for the detonation of the first atomic weapon, in New Mexico. Forty-five years after the test explosion, the chemists, nuclear physicists and mathematicians who had collaborated on the project were brought together to reflect on its significance. Palmer says that he was struck by the humanity, the moral anguish of those who wrestle with the meaning of their participation in the event. You cannot 'hate' any one of them, he said – but the most chilling message in the documentary of this reflective gathering came from a mathematician who said:

'The day before we pushed the button on that nuclear weapon, we had done calculations to indicate there was a small but very real possibility that when we set it off there would be an instant incineration of the entire envelope of oxygen surrounding the earth, thus snuffing out life on earth.' Then he says, 'Still, we went ahead and pushed the button.'[6]

[5] Robert Brungs, 'Mixed Blessings: Can Ethics Determine the Middle Ground Between Science and Religion?' *Universitas*, 19, 2 (Winter, 1994), p. 16.
[6] Parker J. Palmer, 'The Violence of Our Knowledge: Toward a Spirituality of Higher Education,' the Michael Keenan Memorial Lecture, St. Thomas More College, University of Saskatchewan, October, 1993.

Reflecting on the manner in which such a moment of history is to be interpreted, Palmer noted that we have become 'so deeply imbued with the idea that truth lies in "experimentation" that we are willing to experiment with the entire planet as a laboratory in order to fulfill our concept of truth.'[7] How chilling. he said, that our very concept of *truth* can lead to self-destruction. The 'work' of those who fathomed the energy potential in atomic nuclei and who fashioned what they perceived to be the ultimate weapon seemed to be justified by their intention and the particularly dire situation faced by the world community.

Following World War Two, as evidenced in the Nuremberg Trials, the world community contemplated with horror some of the applications of newly-developed technologies. Since then, the capacity to know horror at atrocities has been dulled. They have been 'tamed' to the point of seeming normal and within the parameters of daily life.

Integrity in Work

Work becomes increasingly 'human' to the extent that it is truthful in being an expression of the integral body-person and is able to be ordered to the praise of God. Then it contributes both to the becoming of the person as co-creator in relationship to God and to the becoming of the universe. In his earthly salvific work, Jesus witnessed to this integral quality of co-creative labor. He learned a trade, and because he knew the work-life of his Galilean contemporaries, he was able to reveal the intimacies of God-life and salvation in terms of home and marketplace: fishing, baking bread, collecting taxes, seeding fields, harvesting, and caring for the sick. His parables drew images from an array of daily pursuits in first-century Palestine – from the care of commercial vineyards to the search for fine pearls. Indirectly, the parables affirm that the dignity of work springs from persons, not from particular sophistication of apparatus or extravagant monetary gain (the latter shown in parables concerning 'bigger barns' and the vintner who goes out to hire laborers at succeeding hours of the day).

Since he was a participant in the work situations of his day,

---

[7] Parker Palmer, 'The Violence of Our Knowledge' Lecture.

Jesus was able to reveal *the unguessed potential in the material universe*. He approached ordinary labor with reverence but without undue concern. In the encyclical *Veritatis Splendor* (The Splendor of Truth), Pope John Paul II stresses that human actions are capable of being directed to God when they are in harmony with Natural Law – that reasoned participation in the Eternal Law which respects the integrity of every being in the universe – and when they manifest a humble recognition of the limitations involved. There is a paradox here. When the 'work of one's hands' is carried out in the context of respect for the integrity of every being, two seemingly incompatible truths of reality are evident: 1) the limitations of created beings; and 2) the potential within honest limitations that can be realized in ways surpassing ordinary logical calculation.

The Gospels abound with examples. Jesus opened Peter and his companions to a potential in 'fishing' that far exceeded their expectations. Within the limitations of lake, boat and nets, the miraculous catch of fish enclosed the greatest harvest of their lives, but it surpassed their delight in 153 netted fish. Increment by increment, Jesus led them to see a far deeper meaning in their labor. Peter's preparatory work of local commercial fishing would be brought to completion far beyond the Sea of Galilee, The dignity of his labor has been assumed into a universal meaning: the insignia worn on the papal ring is the 'sign of the fisherman.' Every human work is called beyond its *obviousness* to be an expression of the entire body-person, moving toward fulfillment in relationship and divine image, toward a communion of persons.

That is why the perfect expression and summation of work is found in the Eucharist. Through every moment of his earthly existence Jesus was working toward the culmination of his earthly mission: his perpetual Self-gift in the body and the blood. The work of his entire life tended toward and attained its final meaning in the Paschal Mystery, the accomplishment of salvific work that unfolds as one event from the Last Supper through the resurrection into perpetuity. When he was challenged for curing a sick man on the sabbath, Jesus assured those who were disturbed: 'My Father goes on working, and so do I' (Jn. 5:17). All of his earthly life progressed to that culmination that he named his 'hour.'

Hans Urs von Balthasar theologizes about the twofold content of the Last Supper: the 'self-distribution' of Christ at the meal, and 'the serving mind-set which he established, in a perspective of eschatological fulfilment.'[8] Christ's gift at the Last Supper does not merely refer to a 'pure presence of language' nor the 'reification' of Christ's bodilyness. It is

> the indivisible unity of his self-gift 'for the multitude' – and this gift is not just an 'attitude' but an integrally human enactment carried out precisely by virtue of the bodiliness which discloses in a deeper way the identity between the person of Jesus and his soteriological function. In that function, he is at once a disposer (an institutor of the Eucharist, the new covenant in his blood) and the disposed of (in obedience to the hour, when, at the Father's disposition, he will be handed over.)[9]

Balthasar thus names two characteristics of Christ's culminating work that identify the ultimate meaning of *all* human work. Each integral act of work discloses, through the body, the identity of the person who works and the possibility of the act's being a participation in the saving work of Christ. When that is true, a worker 1) 'disposes,' or spends his/her talents and energies to contribute in some way to the fulfillment of the entire universe; and 2) is 'disposed of' personally in self-gift in obedient response to the lifetime received from the Father. Work involves the entire body-person and participates in the 'splendor of truth' when it is lived out as gift that is expressed in one's body and blood. In terms of the Last Supper, each act of work takes its dignity from the person who expresses self-gift through it, who says with Christ: this is my body, given for you. The disposing of personal work in the ongoing co-creation of the universe, and loving, personal 'being disposed of' in self-gift have their *raison d'être* in Christ who personally, bodily concretized this unity as he entered his passion. Under signs of bread and wine he *disposed of himself*; through the washing of feet he *disposed service*. Bending beneath the scourge, carrying his cross, enduring the agony of unmitigated death, he culminated the work of salvation.

[8] Hans Urs von Balthasar, *Mysterium Paschale*, trans. Aidan Nichols (Grand Rapids, MI, 1990), p. 96.
[9] Hans Urs von Balthasar, *Mysterium Paschale*, p. 97.

Some would diminish his passion by comparing its brevity with extended cancer, AIDS, and paraplegic types of suffering. Every person has a unique cross, a personal possibility of 'making up for what is wanting in the sufferings of Christ' (a participation that can come only from the love response of each individual). As Balthasar reflects, however, Jesus' whole existence 'was, from the start, interiorly identical with the Cross,'[10] even though his 'hour' and the 'powers of darkness' were distinct in time and place from all that preceded them. What the New Testament writings describe in terms of trouble and terror must be understood, says Balthasar, in the context of Christ's 'draining the chalice (of eschatological wrath)....'[11] Through the hypostatic union of divinity and humanity, Jesus Christ assumed *universal* guilt. Out of love, he did not distinguish himself from the anguish of sinners, threatened with the loss of God. Assuming *all* sinners' pain of loss, 'he experiences the anxiety and horror which they by rights should have known for themselves.'[12] Christ was totally willing to be expended, 'disposed of' in his humanity as co-sufferer for all.

The accumulated knowledge now available for understanding the psychological as well as the spiritual and physical depths of even *one* person's suffering of guilt, anxiety, terror, and physical aberrations because of sin, gives some insight into the meaning of Jesus' entering into the paschal work of redemption, taking upon himself the 'sin of the world.' Son of God and Son of Mary, he simultaneously summed up in his person a divine love for the Father and a comprehension of all human consciousness. In his *kenosis* (total self-emptying in Self-gift), he made himself disposable for assuming the wounded reality of all humankind and its eschatological destiny. Pope John Paul II, in the conclusion of *On Human Work* links human sweat and toil with Christ's carrying of the cross. By enduring difficult labor in union with Christ crucified, a worker 'collaborates with the Son of God for the redemption of humanity' (#27). In the present age, carrying the cross involves a taking up of the 'sin of the world,' often as it is concretized in indiscriminately employed

[10] Hans Urs von Balthasar, *Mysterium Paschale*, p. 93. See also p. 94.
[11] Hans Urs von Balthasar, *Mysterium Paschale*, p. 101. He cites Jn. 18:11; 2 Cor. 5:21; Rom. 8:3; Gal. 3:13ff; and Jn. 12:31, 16:11.
[12] Hans Urs von Balthasar, *Mysterium Paschale*, p. 104.

forms of technology that offer enormous economic gains for only a small portion of humanity. Injustices prove a constant challenge to the integrity of workers who are responsible for the gifts of the earth.

When the technological breakthroughs of the 1950s began to revolutionize communications industries, the combination of efficient techniques with high speed affected workers. In some instances workers were asked to perform accustomed jobs as a means of 'putting in timeclock hours' when they knew that the work of their hands would be meaningless. To illustrate this: in a large United States city, skilled workers who assembled frames of type and headlines for a major newspaper were replaced by high-tech cylindrical machines. In order that workers be retained and receive wages, the workers came daily at the appointed time, and worked their shift, setting up the heavy frames of type in the accustomed manner – only to break them apart at the end of the work day while in another part of the industry the 'real' presses rolled. In order to solve an immediate problem there was a by-passing of the workers' human dignity and their relatedness to the work of their hands.

Edmond Barbotin speaks of the hand as the organ of our relations with the world. Hands are mediating points between a person and the larger world. While many of the body's organs are beyond control of the will, the hand is 'wholly at the disposal of my freedom as it endeavors to transform the world.'[13] The hand expresses the whole spiritual body-being and carries out the intention of the person. Every tool which extends the body is in relationship to the hand as its source. It is through the hand, as a major organ of transformation, that one takes hold of the world. Techniques employed by the hand express *us* and our relation-ships: the whole person can be described in terms of grasping, enfolding, striking, pushing away. It is not surprising that anthropomorphic descriptions of God's work utilize the imagery of hands (perhaps the most universally recognized image of this being Michelangelo's 'hand of God' stretched out to the hand of Adam). Barbotin writes that a person's hand is marked by tools and all things touched. Hands are strengthened, painfully fur-rowed or refined by things.

[13] Edmond Barbotin, *The Humanity of Man*, p. 197.

When a person adapts to a new kind of work, he 'gets his hand in,' as the idiom intuitively expresses it.... All the repeated efforts, all the wounds or blows received, leave their living testimony in the flesh. I can read a trade and a human life in a worker's hand. Tell me what your hand is like, and I will tell you who you are.[14]

Even as a hand contacts the world, it is contacted. Always it is the complete person who is present through the hand, so that in the course of work, when a hand is burned or mangled, the entire body-person is affected, not just the 'organ of work.' Mind, emotions, vision and intention are closely linked, revealing artistic and contemplative endeavors in addition to practical pursuits. Works of the hand reflect works of the heart. A few decades ago, the well-preserved desert grave of a Neanderthal was discovered. What amazed archeologists: the body had been buried in a fetal position and it had been buried with flowers. Thought, emotion, and some conviction about death's meaning were all expressed through hands that arranged the corpse in that manner, gathered flowers and placed them with the body. The find in the desert caused archeologists to reevaluate the level of human capacities that were 'at work' in the Neanderthal period.

Human Work Requires Balance

The poignant Scripture texts chosen for the liturgy of the Easter Vigil sequentially interpret the working out of salvation, from creation through the work of redemption. It is significant that the creation account of Genesis 1, resounding with the conviction that creation is good, and in summary 'indeed, very good,' concludes with divine 'rest.' The image of divine rest contains no suggestion of anthropomorphic need to restore strength after labor. Rather, it suggests a contemplative affirmation, a celebratory 'letting be' that complements Christ's saying, 'My Father goes on working, and so do I' (Jn. 5:17).

Human work, in the sense of completing tasks, is not an ultimate goal for the human person. Neither is human ingenuity destined to find perfect fulfillment in some 'workless existence' on earth, a nearly continuous sabbath given to play. The deca-

[14] Edmond Barbotin, *The Humanity of Man*, p. 196.

dent period of Roman civilization in which, on average, half the days of the year were holidays for government-provided bread and circuses, is a reminder that explicit violence and dissipation quickly fill the void created by excessive leisure. Work involves a paradox: governments traditionally have imposed arduous labor as a punishment for criminal acts; yet those who are deprived of challenging work often experience a depression that influences their sense of self-worth.

Genesis 3 already signals an imbalance in human work that is the result of sin and is closely associated with discord and imbalance between women and men. Blame, mistrust, deception and subjugation marred the co-responsibilities of male and female following original sin. Historically, the visible, outward, controlling and 'doing' aspects of work have been associated with males, while the invisible, inward-directed, and 'receptive' aspects of work have been associated with females. The former have traditionally been esteemed as superior, as constituting the 'work' that creates the future of the universe; the latter have been considered inferior and subordinate. As a result, among so-called developed nations, there is keen competition between women and men for securing prestigious and lucrative positions. Creative and developmental aspects of sporting events also reveal a cut-throat competition – a development which reached new intensity in the Olympic games of 1994 and the ensuing figure-skating competitions. In a sin-conditioned world, work bears the woundedness of woman-man relations and the imbalance between creative labor and contemplative rest.

The meaning of work is intimately connected to the mystery of time. While the historical chronology of a person's life can be measured, it is but a momentary flick within the existence of the universe – whose chronological breadth exceeds the human capacity to know or measure. Where any individual's brief life-span falls within this immense, horizonless unfolding will determine the kinds of work to be lived out bodily. In his *Confessions* Augustine grappled with the meaning of time, the meaning of our saying 'past, present, and future' when, in reality, the past no longer has an existence, nor has the future. We can only remember the past and anticipate the future. It is only the immediate moment that can be lived – that which we call the 'present' and is available for work. It is total gift, either to be received and lived with gratitude, or rejected, perhaps squandered. It will never 'be' again. The concatenation of possibilities, relationships, circumstances and personal preparedness in each *now* is unique and unrepeatable. A playful caricature in the series called 'Family Circus' proves to be a contemporary parable. It portrays a little girl explaining time to her younger brother: 'Yesterday's the past, tomorrow's the future, but today is a GIFT. That's why it's called the present.'

The Work of Justice

Beginning with Pope Leo XIII's landmark encyclical, *Rerum Novarum*, written in the late nineteenth century, the Roman Catholic Church has emphasized that all questions regarding work are to be understood in terms of the human person and the family. In successive documents following that encyclical, Church teaching has clarified the importance of justice for workers and justice in the utilization and distribution of earth's resources. It is impossible to elaborate here on the accumulated insights of *Quadragesimo Anno*, *Centesimus Annus*, *Gaudium et Spes*, and *Laborem Exercens*, which together convey and apply to new situations the rich heritage of Church teaching concerning the dignity of workers and the rightful use of earth's resources.

All labor exists for the sake of the person, the family and the responsible development of the earth, not simply for the benefit of private gain on the part of those who manipulate others and hoard vast quantities of earth's resources. There is nothing sentimental about a faith understanding of toil. It takes into account monotony, anxiety, and danger, along with a concern for just wages that permit a way of life consonant with human dignity. The community of earth's peoples has reached a significant turning point in responsibility for resources. There is new urgency in seeing the relationship between divinely-given stewardship and the reality of limitation. While there is increased capacity for productivity, there is a concurrent press among the developed nations to curtail the world's population by attaching economic aid to the requirement of mass programs of artificial contraception, abortion and sterilization. Media campaigns attempt to persuade large segments of society that the solution for injustices in the distribution of wealth lies in severe reduction of human births. Then the *person*, for whom work exists, becomes the victim of inadequate or skewed planning. World planner Buckminster Fuller once observed that whenever we do not know how to solve a problem, we kill.

The lack of meaningful work results in the loss of self-esteem and the inability to make an honest personal contribution through living out God-given talents. Frustration impels many to violence as a means of claiming a portion of this world's goods. The problem is compounded by those who claim that animals have 'rights' which can even supersede human rights. The 'Wildlands Project' projected for implementation in the United States would return from one-third to one-half the nation to wilderness within approximately fifty years. In critiquing a final draft document for the United Nations International Conference on Population and Development (held in Cairo, September, 1994) Pope John Paul II noted the inevitable link between expanding population and the larger global environment. He cited *Centesimus Annus*:

> Human ingenuity seems to be directed more toward limiting, suppressing or destroying the sources of life – including recourse to abortion, which unfortunately is so widespread in the world – than toward defending and opening up the possibility of life (#39).

Commenting on the tendency to blame environmental problems on population growth, the Pope noted that the matter is more complex than that. The natural environment is endangered when there is a lack of restriction on industrial and production processes and when the developed nations are irresponsible in matters of consumption and waste.[15] The Holy See's contribution to issues of economic and demographic concern, said the Pope, would consist in bringing an ethical perspective, from a conviction that only a respect for, and a conformity with, God's providential plan could bring genuine equality, unity and peace. There is a close link between treating future generations as products of our ingenuity and imagination, and the desecration of the earth and nonhuman creatures that inhabit it.

[15] See Pope John Paul II, 'Population Conference Draft Document Criticized,' *Origins*, 23, 41 (March 31, 1994), p. 718.

Ultimately, work is to be an act of creative love and every honest work has the potential of being a prayerful response to trinitarian love. It is in that light that we explore what it means to 'pray the body.'

10

Praying the Body

IN liturgical prayer the Holy Spirit is frequently invoked 1) to remain as personal, indwelling guest, and 2) to renew the face of the earth. Each invocation touches upon bodilyness. St. Paul calls the lived bodies of the baptized 'temples of the Holy Spirit.' He writes in 1 Corinthians 3:16–17: 'Didn't you realise that you were God's temple and that the Spirit of God was living among you? If anybody should destroy the temple of God, God will destroy him, because the temple of God is sacred; and you are that temple.' He says again in the same letter: 'Your body, you know, is the temple of the Holy Spirit, who is in you since you received him from God' (1 Cor. 6:19). Based on his personal encounter with the Risen Lord, he spoke experientially of Christ's intimate identification with the embodied Church. This underscores the extraordinary dignity of the human body as a sacred place of worship, although it may be desecrated from within or without. For those united to Christ in the Holy Spirit, the body is a living, mobile location of prayer, a living monstrance for Christ. St. Paul dwells on the meaning of the body of Christ, his risen reality and sacramental presence (see 1 Cor. 11); his close communion with individuals (see 1 Cor. 6) and the whole community (see Eph. 1:22–23).

In previous chapters attention was given to the profound interrelationships between the lived body and the rest of the created universe, and the enduring influence of even the slightest human act within the space/time continuum. It was noted that the material universe is in a constant process of interchange, so that Teilhard de Chardin could say that our bodies are not part of the universe that we possess totally, but the whole of the universe that we possess partially. Whatever in creation participates in the splendor of *the truths of reality* is brought into the saving pattern of Christ's redemptive, effective presence. George Maloney writes:

Quantum physicists speak no longer of created matter as a solid mass. They speak more and more in the language of mystics. Everything in the cosmos is inter-connected and moves in a harmonious wholeness. Each part has its proper place within the universe. Each creature depends on and gives support to all the others in one great body, all of which in the belief of Christianity is being created in and through God's Word with the cooperation of human beings. How beautifully this is brought out in Psalm 104: Yahweh, what variety you have created ... you keep renewing the world (Ps. 104: 24–25, 30).[1]

In Romans 8 St. Paul asserts that the whole earth is groaning, waiting for the revelation of our bodies. Within creation, the vivid interchanges of matter that course through the human body signal the capacity of the human person to participate in all of creation, drawing it into conscious praise. In prayer, one who is aware that the body is a partial centering of the entire universe is able, by extension, to bring the entire universe into praise. Paul urges: 'Pray all the time' (Eph. 6:18), 'and never say or do anything except in the name of the Lord Jesus ...' (Col. 3:17). Because we are *embodied* it is possible to bring all of creation intimately into the prayer of praise, thanksgiving and reparation.

Francis of Assisi, perhaps more than any other follower of Christ, knew and lived this mystery intimately, and non-human creatures responded. Attentive flocks of larks and the subdued wolf of Gubbio are not simply the focus of sentimental legends, perpetuated in order to edify Francis' admirers. They are substantive examples from the lived experience of one who was able to draw creation and specific creatures into his conscious prayer of praise. Francis' Canticle of the Creatures was an expression of his purified capacity to 'give body' to inward prayer. There was nothing sentimental about his severe penances, his prayer in the clefts of wintry mountains, lived out despite frequent illness. Close to death (from dropsy, perhaps leprosy?) he listened to counsel and tempered the severity he had shown to his own body which he had called 'brother ass.' In *God's Fool*, Julien Green

---

[1] George A. Maloney, *The Silence of Surrendering Love: Body, Soul, Spirit Integration* (New York, 1986), p. 15.

ponders Francis' last request to be placed naked on the naked earth in his dying moments, and notes how 'an exaltation of larks' flew low, whirling and singing over the dying man's cell: 'In human memory no one has heard the song of the lark except in the early hours of the morning, rising with the sun. But that evening they left everything behind and came to cry out their love.'[2]

Francis' body was marked with the stigmata, outward sign of Christ's passion, directly relating him to Christ and the entire universe. Honest prayer of praise can best be expressed when there is an integral realization of its splendor and its woundedness, beginning with one's own body. To 'pray the body' requires a prior capacity to receive embodiment as a gift of love. The 'prayed body' integrates reverence, a sacred freedom (which ascetical theology has traditionally called 'detachment'), and the offering of the embodied self as gift.

The senses participate in prayer. It is in Baptism that the embodied person becomes a living temple of the Holy Spirit, a mobile dwelling place of God. Through Baptism, *the body is sacramentalized* and becomes a living outward sign of the Trinity's effective Presence on earth. Fragrant incense is used liturgically to indicate prayer itself, or what is offered in prayer. After the altar, the Gospel book and celebrant are incensed in the Eucharist, the living embodied community is also incensed. In the Mass of Resurrection celebrated for one who has died, the casket is draped with a white cloth, recalling Baptism, and the body is incensed a final time and blessed with holy water. Tertullian, noting how the flesh is the hinge of salvation wrote:

> . . . the flesh is washed in order that the soul may be cleansed; the flesh is anointed in order that the soul may be consecrated; the flesh is signed in order that the soul may be fortified; the flesh is overshadowed by the imposition of the hand in order that the soul may be illumined by the Spirit. The body feeds on the flesh and blood of Christ so that the soul might feast upon God. Therefore, those things which work joins together are not able to be separated in reward.[3]

[2] Julien Green, *God's Fool: The Life and Times of Francis of Assisi*, trans. Peter Heinegg (San Francisco, 1985), p. 271.
[3] Tertullian, *De resurrectione carnis*, 8:6–12.

THE RISEN LORD'S REAL AND CORPOREAL BODY

In the Paschal Mystery, celebrated in the Eucharist, prayer of the body can be probed to its greatest depth. St. Paul writes: '... the bread we break is a communion with the body of Christ' (1 Cor. 10:16). Josef Ernst says that reception of the Eucharist is not simply a vague kind of idealistic union with Christ or table fellowship:

> ... it means a real participation in the body of the Lord such as happens when food is ingested. The apostle is not afraid of the danger of possible magical misunderstanding, though of course this is excluded by the term 'communion' (*koinonia*) with its fundamentally personal connotation. At all events 'the communion of the body of Christ' brought about by the breaking of the bread cannot be thought of realistically enough; this is also shown by the 'baptizing (immersion) into the death of Jesus Christ' (Rom. 6, 3) at baptism, as well as by the comparison with sexual union in marriage (1 Cor. 6, 15).[4]

To the time of St. Augustine, the Church used the term 'mystical body' to mean 'simultaneously and inseparably the eucharistic and the ecclesiological body.'[5] Recently, some theologians tend to minimize the significance of physical acts in themselves. Ernst's assertions about the communion between the real risen body of Christ and the ecclesiological body formed by those baptized in Christ are clearly important. He says that Pauline 'pneumatology' cannot be employed to diminish the reality of Christ's risen body. The Risen Lord's body is pneumatic and mystical, but 'precisely as such, real and corporeal,' says Ernst. 'The fact that there is only one loaf,' St. Paul said, 'means that, though there are many of us, we form a single body because we all have a share in this one loaf' (1 Cor 10:17). The reception of Eucharist is a *communion* between Christ and Christians. This obviates a metaphysical pantheism (which would suggest a direct

---

[4] Josef Ernst, 'Significance of Christ's Eucharistic Body for the Unity of Church and Cosmos,' in *The Breaking of Bread*, eds. Pierre Benoit, Roland Murphy and Bastian Van Iersel (New York, 1969), p. 107.
[5] Josef Ernst, 'Significance of Christ's Eucharistic Body,' p. 108.

equation between the Risen Lord and members of the community). The real, ontic union between Christ and the members of the Church is rooted in a personal decision of faith (see Eph. 2:8), guaranteeing the 'necessary difference' between Christ and those who are in communion with him.[6] It is a love union to be expressed in *diakonia* – service to other persons and the whole of creation. The Letter to the Ephesians states that the Church is to be the means by which the power of healing and redemption are extended to non-human creatures: *'He has put all things under his feet, and made him, as ruler of everything, the head of the Church; which is his body, the fullness of him who fills the whole creation'* (Eph. 1: 22–23). As the Church, Body of Christ, grows into greater union with him, the consecration of the world is taking place. Having saved humanity through his Paschal Self-offering, Christ has given the body of believers the power to extend itself in service. The body of Christ has cosmic perspectives, says Ernst. Cosmic realms are brought into 'the process of unification and recapitulation in Christ, until God is 'all in all'.[7] This is occurring now, in the Eucharist.

The contesting of Christ's real, bodily Presence in the Eucharist is surely not a new phenomenon. It recurs variously throughout the history of the Church. In the late twentieth century, questioning of Christ's Real Presence in the Eucharist is related to a more universal questioning of the reality of his Incarnation. Apart from the full reality of the Incarnation and Christ's enduring resurrected Presence in the Eucharist, Christian 'praying the body' would be superficial. It would simply be a general expression of relationship to the divine, a way of offering praise through the use of embodied art, appreciation for material realities and generous service of others (all having a quality of goodness, but lacking living, personal communion in Christ). When the *corporeal* reality of Christ's life, death and resurrection is open to vague interpretations the basic meaning of Christianity disintegrates. Either Christ's body is enduringly real, or as St. Paul wrote, Christians have been duped:

> ... if Christ has not been raised then our preaching is useless and your believing it is useless; indeed, we are shown up as witnesses

---

[6] See Josef Ernst, 'Significance of Christ's Eucharistic Body,' p. 112.
[7] Josef Ernst, 'Significance of Christ's Eucharistic Body,' p. 116.

who have committed perjury before God, because we swore in evidence before God that he had raised Christ to life. For if the dead are not raised, Christ has not been raised, and if Christ has not been raised, you are still in your sins. And what is more serious, all who have died in Christ have perished. If our hope in Christ has been for this life only, we are the most unfortunate of all people (1 Cor. 15:14–19).

That is why, in depth understanding of the Theology of the Body, the body is discerned as symbolic in its deepest reality, requiring the distinctions discussed above between lesser levels of symbol and Real Symbol. Because the lived body is a person's Real Symbol, we are able bodily to 'say what we mean and mean what we say' in loving response to divine creative love. The greater the integral unity of the person (the outward manifestation bearing the truth of the whole person) the more total the capacity to 'pray the body.' This may also aid in the understanding of physical phenomena that sometimes accompany mystical prayer. Teresa of Avila, for instance, knew extraordinary bodily reactions in her journey into union with God, a journey which she described in the familiar imagery of her day as penetration into the interior castle. She attempted to describe various phenomena experienced in prayer in terms of levitations, locutions, visions and the unique transverberation that marked her heart. It is significant that when she described the 'seventh mansion' or state of mystical marriage with Christ, it seems that extraordinary bodily phenomena had subsided. In the final months of her physical and spiritual suffering, there was a bodily quieting. Whether she was adverting to her enduring mystical marriage, working on financial matters, or struggling with severe physical distress, her whole being *was* in prayer, the outward Real Symbol expressing her total union with Christ.

INCARNATE WORD: ABSOLUTE SYMBOL OF GOD IN THE WORLD

The corporeal *reality* of Jesus Christ's Incarnation, earthly life, Paschal Self-gift and resurrection are the basis of Christian faith and life. Rahner stressed that 'the incarnate word is the absolute symbol of God in the world, filled as nothing else can be with what is symbolized.'[8] His expressive Presence embodies what it signifies. Christ's body is not simply a 'sign' or mere representation as conventional symbols are, nor is it an impersonal natural power. He is the effective Incarnate Presence and Revelation of God in the world. When he came to the Last Supper, his whole being was at-one, so that his body was Real Symbol of total Self-gift to the Father, to those at table with him, as well as to all who would later come to receive him. At the Supper he bodily enacted the single choice of his whole being: Self-gift in perpetual love through and beyond death. He told those gathered with him exactly what he was doing: becoming complete Self-gift for the advantage of others because of his relationship with the Father. Time cannot touch this. The core of Christ's existence is his relationship/presence with the Father and the Holy Spirit, precisely as bridegroom of the Church. The *Constitution on the Sacred Liturgy* of the Second Vatican Council lists the number of ways in which Christ is present in the Church: in the sacraments, in his Word, in the community gathered in prayer and song, in the person of the celebrant at the eucharistic celebration, 'but especially in the eucharistic species' (see Ch. I).

What expresses a person most fully is the person fully present, capable of effective self-gift. When, in the Eucharist, Christ's permanent Self-gift is expressed in the words 'This is my body,' it means *himself*, tangible and truly present. His sacramental gift, 'This is my blood' is his entire Self-gift as source of life given for us. The human capacity for self-gift reaches its fullest potential in the Eucharist, where Person is given as sacramental food and drink.

All external gifts are ways of extending the gift of self, but nothing replaces the human embodied image of divine identity: 'I shall be there with you as who I am shall I be there.' The most profound gift is to be given bodily for another *as completely and appropriately as possible*. Marital sexual intercourse *can* be the integral expression of such self-gift in a faithful marriage, but it is always a limited, temporary manner of mutual self-gift. The most profound handing over of self in the body is to give one's body and blood to be received as food and drink in a forever-gift. Most

---

[8] Karl Rahner, 'The Theology of the Symbol,' p. 237.

of Jesus' followers withdrew from him when he promised such Self-gift, unable to make the leap of faith required (although he had already opened them to a totally new understanding of miraculous food in the multiplication of loaves and fishes). They lacked faith in his capacity to bring ordinary realities of eating and drinking into a previously unguessed dimension of possibility. His first public miracle at Cana was a preparation for ultimate, perpetual Self-gift. Benedict Ashley writes:

> Thus, in trying to understand how intimately personal Christ's presence is in the Eucharist, we ought not to think of this merely as the presence of someone facing us in dialogue, but we must retain the fact that he is present to offer himself as our food and drink.[9]

Christ's Real Presence in the Eucharist is his personal Presence given as food and drink. That is why the Blessed Sacrament is reverenced and retained in a holy place, not treated as ordinary bread or a mere sign. The enduring question is: how can this be? It is disputed today whether the term 'substance,' used in traditional theologizing about the Eucharist, is adequate for naming the basic sacramental change of elements from ordinary bread and wine to the personal Self-gift of Christ. The philosophical and theological use of 'substance' has proved problematic precisely 1) because the word has acquired various connotations over the centuries, and 2) because the scientific analysis of matter can make the term 'substance' incommensurate for describing what formerly was intended to mean the *reality* of bread and wine and the *reality* of the body and blood.

The term 'substance' is used variously in the physical sciences. For many today, primary reality is attributed only to *natural* units in their properties and behaviors – not to those which are formed by human hands, such as bread and wine, nor to those which involve personal presence. Philosophers may use 'substance' to mean an 'object' over against the realm of human experience. From what we know of matter, the term 'substance' can also be used to designate the recognizable unity of an organism that is living and in process. 'Substance' does not depend upon a certain size or position in space. The minute cell that

---

[9] Benedict Ashley, *Theologies of the Body*, p. 663.

comes into existence at the conception of a child is the same *substantial person* who will later be visibly present and acknowledged as a newborn, a youth, and later a seasoned adult.

TRANSUBSTANTIAL CHANGE

In the Eucharist, the Risen Lord is *substantially* present, in Self-gift. While the term 'substance' has come into various forms of common usage, some of which have just been described, until such time as the word is superseded by a more apt term, it remains a suitable basic term to be used in explaining the change that occurs in the Mass when bread and wine are consecrated and *are substantially changed into the body and blood of Christ given in Self-gift.* All lower levels of symbolic meaning in bread and wine are incorporated into the Real Symbol of the living Christ's body and blood. Their intrinsic symbolic meanings of sustaining life, promoting well-being and communion are not lost in the transubstantial change. Jesus had prepared his followers well concerning the conventional and natural symbolic meaning of bread. The Gospels relate how he had been tempted to turn stones into bread in order to appease his hunger, and how he had refused the suggestion (not only did the temptation arise from an evil source, but it also proposed a transformation that would have violated the meaning of stone, good in its own intrinsic meaning). Later Jesus queried: if a child asks for bread, would his father hand him a stone? (see Matt. 7:9), indicating the inappropriateness of such a response. Only after showing the unguessed potential of bread in its capacity to sustain life, to provide well-being and a sense of community, did Jesus change it *substantially* into his Self-gift. The outward phenomena remained, but were caught up in the Real Symbol of his living body. In Eucharist, the elements brought to consecration no longer *say* bread and wine, but the Self-gift of Christ present.

Today, Christians are able to know the properties of matter and the human body in new ways. Since the human body is not identified with a single instance of its changing state, *size* and *shape* are not the determiners of personal body presence. This is clearly discernible in daily experience. Likewise, Christ's glorified body, sacramentally present, does not require a certain size of unleavened bread or a certain amount of 'space' to be truly present. What were formally ordinary bread and wine are transformed in their *reality*; they now sacramentalize Christ in Self-gift because of the words spoken *in persona Christi* by the presiding priest. More adequate terms than 'transubstantiation' (change of substance) may one day be used to name the crucial ontological change that occurs in the Eucharist, but the *reality* will remain, whatever future terms may be used to denote the transformation from bread and wine into the authentic personal presence and Self-gift of Christ.

What was discussed earlier concerning the continual exchanges among bodies and elements suggests a deeper understanding of the 'field of presence' that anyone enters in coming into the immediacy of the Blessed Sacrament (knowingly or unknowingly). If electrons from our bodies are, in statistical probability, now at the far reaches of the Milky Way, what must this mean concerning the sacramental presence of the Risen Christ in the Eucharist? There is an intimate union among the basic doctrines of faith which touch upon the bodily reality of Christ. If his Incarnation, his passion, death, and resurrection, and eucharistic Self-gift are understood merely as 'symbolic representation' (or mythic assertion or ritual for empowerment among community members), the Real Presence is not acknowledged. At various times in Christian history there have been radical misunderstandings of the fundamental meaning of the Eucharist – sometimes in graphically time-bound physicalist manner (e.g. the Berengarian heresy); sometimes through considering Eucharist a mere commemorative service, a way of bonding members of the community in Jesus' name.

Christ's personal Self-gift in the body and the blood is the prime reference for understanding every human person's potential for bodily self-gift. The creation accounts of Genesis indicate that woman and man are created in a communion of persons, called to be mutual gifts to one another. This is always a bodily reality. John Paul II says:

> This is the body: a witness to creation as a fundamental gift, and so a witness to Love as the source from which this same giving springs. Masculinity-femininity – namely sex – is the original sign of a creative donation and of an awareness on the part of man,

male-female, of a gift lived so to speak in an original way.... That beatifying 'beginning' of man's being and existing, as male and female, is connected with the revelation and discovery of the meaning of the body, which can be called 'nuptial.'[10]

'Praying the body' takes its central significance as nuptial from Christ's Self-gift in and through the body. All derivative forms of body prayer (e.g. kneeling, bowing, lifting up one's hands, processing, singing, sacred dancing) are extensions of this basic meaning. The nuptial meaning of the body provides a basic criterion for reflecting upon and evaluating post-conciliar liturgical revisions and practices which expressly involve bodily enactment. When liturgical life is at-one with the eucharistic Self-gift of Christ, it is authentic. If it is perceived primarily as needing to draw attention to self or to show personal empowerment, it becomes dissociated from the fundamental meaning of 'praying the body.' St. Paul, however, admonished the early Church communities to 'pray always' in word and work – and this extension of liturgical prayer into home and marketplace takes its meaning from the same source: body as expression of self-gift. Pruning trees or maneuvering an automobile across expressways can be body prayers.

St. Paul noted how creation groans for the revelation of the body in its truth. Two divergent views of body and earth can distort an incarnational-eucharistic approach to stewardship: 1) a worshipful attitude which considers the earth worthy of divine veneration or treats the natural earth as the ultimate reality (often derived from contemporizing ancient goddess worship); and 2) a utilitarian perspective, extending scientific/technical ingenuity to the re-creation of earth and its inhabitants according to the insights of the present age. While many past tribes and cultures venerated the earth, personalizing its powerful, mysterious forces, they did not know the Revelation of the Creator. They saw from afar, as it were, but they knew the importance of respecting creation.

Following a relentless abuse of the earth and its resources, humanity is currently recognizing that a devastating backlash is occurring. The gifts of water, air, and food now often have to be feared, not because they possess a divine retaliatory power, but

[10] Pope John Paul II, *The Original Unity*, p. 110.

because they have been wounded in their natural potential and utilized in isolation from their ultimate Source. To pray the body is a concrete expression of praise and thanks – but it is also a way of 'filling up what is wanting in the sufferings of Christ,' and it is to this which we now turn. What is the place of suffering, dying and death within a Theology of the Body?

II

Human Suffering

DESPITE its foundational significance within Christian faith, suffering transcends any facile explanation. Pope John Paul II in his apostolic letter *On the Christian Meaning of Human Suffering* says that although the revelation of divine love, that 'ultimate source of the meaning of everything that exists,'[1] is the only answer to the *why* of suffering, the latter still retains its character as mystery:

> ... we are conscious of the insufficiency and inadequacy of our explanations. Christ causes us to enter into the mystery and to discover the 'why' of suffering, as far as we are capable of grasping the sublimity of divine love.[2]

Briefly, John Paul II asserts that 1) human suffering remains a mystery; 2) its core meaning is to be found in the revelation of divine love; and 3) our entry into the mystery of suffering is linked with the capacity, as John Paul says, 'to grasp' the sublimity of divine love. Rarely in the post-modern milieu is there public advertence to the 'sublimity of divine love.' So, it is not surprising that the world community, inundated with suffering, spawns novel ways of attempting to eliminate it from personal experience. Personal suffering is perceived by many to be an outright evil to be avoided, and deliverance from it a *right* to be defended. Within the context of faith seeking understanding, however, Christianity affirms that the *meaning* of suffering can be found only in divine love made visible and tangible in Jesus Christ.

The word 'suffer' is derived from two Latin roots: *ferre* (to bear) and *sub* (under). Helen Luke suggests that 'undercarriage' (that part of a vehicle which carries weight above the wheels) is a

---

[1] Pope John Paul II, *On the Christian Meaning of Human Suffering*, Vatican trans. (Boston, MA, issued February 11, 1984), #13.
[2] John Paul II, *On the Christian Meaning of Human Suffering*, #13.

fitting image for suffering. Terms such as grief, affliction and depression have the sense of *pressing down*, she says, but 'Only when we suffer in the full sense of the word do we *carry* the weight.'[3] Christ's invitation to each person to 'take up his cross and follow me' (Mk. 8:34) and his assurance 'my yoke is easy and my burden light' (Matt. 11:30) underscore this meaning of bearing up, of taking weight upon oneself.

THE MYSTERY OF SUFFERING

In the context of imprisonment, the Letter to the Colossians describes St. Paul's identification with Christ's sufferings: 'It makes me happy to suffer for you, as I am suffering now, and in my own body to do what I can to make up all that has still to be undergone by Christ for the sake of his body, the Church' (Col. 1:24). Paul understood his sharing in the sufferings of Christ to be for the sake of others. He was very specific in saying that he carried this weight in his body as *sarx* ('flesh,' that is, his body considered in its weaknesses). Writing earlier to the Romans, Paul had said that suffering brings patience, which in turn brings perseverance, from which hope springs – a hope that is not deceptive because it derives from the Holy Spirit, the Person-Gift poured into our hearts (see Rom. 5:3–5).

Because of embodiment, *every* human experience has corporeal dimensions, but this is particularly true of suffering, whether it be physical, spiritual, mental, or emotional. 'In my flesh,' says Paul, 'I complete Christ's afflictions.' The Gospels repeatedly refer to the sufferings of Jesus. When Mary presents him in the temple, a few weeks after his birth, she receives Simeon's difficult blessing: her child will be a sign that is rejected, a dividing point for the 'rise and fall' of many in Israel. At this early stage Mary was already named into co-suffering: her own soul would be pierced 'so that the secret thoughts of many may be laid bare' (Lk. 2:35). There was a clear indication that Mary would be the first, most intimate sharer in Jesus' afflictions. She would not be spared from the anguished grappling with the mystery of suffering. The limited number of Gospel passages that

---

[3] Helen Luke, *Old Age* (New York, 1987), p. 103.

refer to Mary consistently speak of her unique call to mature co-suffering with Christ.

The infancy narratives in Luke and Matthew illustrate this pattern: the dangers and misunderstandings opened through her Annunciation fiat; the difficult circumstances of giving birth in the habitat of animals; the necessity of fleeing in order to save the life of her child; the perils of being a refugee in a foreign land; and the responsibility of finding a lost child. When Jesus initiated his public life, she risked 'calling him out' at Cana. She also knew the anguish of having neighbors in Nazareth attempt to lynch him by throwing him over a cliff; and later she experienced her relatives' judgment that he was mad and needed to have his public activities curbed.

Jesus did not praise his Mother simply because she had borne and nourished him from her own body. Long before the Church confirmed her title of *Theotokos*, Mary heard her Son identify as his 'mother' those who heard the word of God and kept it. The early faith community recalled her faithful stance beneath the cross and her presence in the Upper Room, awaiting the coming of the Holy Spirit. Exemplifying St. Paul's statement about completing 'what is lacking in the afflictions of Christ,' Mary (according to the Gospels) knew an embodied suffering that was a share in Christ's salvific suffering.

How is it possible for ordinary humans to share in Christ's sufferings? In his total Self-gift, Christ, the God-man, procured universal salvation for all who would receive it. There was nothing 'lacking' in his salvific effectiveness. The meaning of 'completion' is found in the mutual sharing of human and *divine* salvific love. It is the mutual love-impelled 'under-bearing' that is significant. The mystics throughout Christian history have emphasized the privilege of being able to share in Christ's sufferings. In the Epilogue of *Story of a Soul: The Autobiography of St. Thérèse of Lisieux*, it is recalled how Thérèse said shortly before her death:

> 'Do not be troubled, little sisters, if I suffer very much and if you see in me, as I have already said to you, no sign of joy at the moment of death. Our Lord really died as a Victim of Love, and see what His agony was!' And in July she said: 'Our Lord died on the Cross in anguish, and yet His was the most beautiful death of

love. To die of love does not mean to die in transports. I tell you frankly, it appears to me that this is what I am experiencing.'[4]

It has been noted above that there is a growing tendency to equate animal and human life. In certain nations this is manifest in legal efforts to secure 'animal rights,' and to protect non-human species and their fertility while attempting to restrict human procreation. This blurring of animal and human life also brings confusion to the necessary distinctions between human pain, suffering and death and the pain/death of animals. Concomitantly, there are efforts to avoid all forms of suffering – and when that fails, to eliminate the sufferer, whether human or animal. For example, the lawyer representing Dr. Jack Kevorkian (a United States leader in the campaign to legalize physician-assisted suicide) has stated that his client is basically seeking from the courts an extension of the United States Bill of Rights: *the right not to suffer.*

When animals are struggling with severe, irreversible pain, it is a *humane* act to hasten their death, precisely because there is no possibility of their choosing a conscious participation in Christ's salvific afflictions. In the Old Covenant, numerous animals had been sacrificed in atonement for sins, with the hope of effecting renewed relationship with God. When Jesus Christ, the one redemptive Paschal Lamb offered himself, the animal sacrifices were forever transcended. The Letter to the Hebrews states:

Bulls' blood and goats' blood are useless for taking away sins, and this is what he said, on coming into the world:

You who wanted no sacrifice or oblation,
prepared a body for me.
You took no pleasure in holocausts or sacrifices for sin;
then I said,
just as I was commanded in the scroll of the book.
'God, here I am! I am coming to obey your will!' ...

And this *will* was for us to be made holy by the *offering* of his *body* made once and for all by Jesus Christ (Heb. 10:4–7, 10).

When the distinction is lost between human and animal life,

[4] Thérèse of Lisieux, *Story of a Soul: The Autobiography of St. Thérèse of Lisieux*, trans. John Clarke, 2nd ed. (Washington, D.C., 1976), p. 269.

suffering is reduced to a natural evil that is to be avoided at all cost. The absence of belief in a transcendent Creator, who invites each human person to an eternal relationship, makes such a reduction seem feasible because suffering seems to lack any intrinsic meaning.

Pope John Paul II says that suffering 'seems to be particularly *essential to the nature of man*,'[5] and proper to human transcendence, a manifestation of the depth proper only to the human person. It belongs to the mysterious call to go beyond the self. Victor Frankl's observation in *Man's Search for Meaning* has become almost proverbial – the human person can bear intense suffering if it is perceived to be meaningful. The *meaning* of suffering, revealed in Christ, changes the possibility of 'bearing under' the diverse causes of suffering. Christ not only taught the necessity of taking up one's cross, but also dignified with his respectful response those persons who endured sufferings which others would consider repulsive: e.g. the ranting, possessed man who dwelt among the tombs, and the lepers with their severely ravaged flesh. If there is no perceived meaning in suffering, two options appear reasonable: either to eliminate the suffering by any means available, or when no relief is available, to eliminate the sufferer. Thérèse of Lisieux, who experienced spiritual aridity and temptations against faith in her intense terminal sufferings underscored this. She said to Mother Agnes:

'What would become of me if God did not give me courage? A person does not know what this is unless he experiences it. No, it has to be experienced!' She even apologized when she cried out with pain: 'What a grace it is to have faith! If I had no faith, I would have inflicted death on myself without hesitating a moment!'[6]

ELIMINATION OF THE SUFFERER

Telecasts that focus on international wars and disasters of all kinds are punctuated by advertisements for products that promise instant relief from personal pain and suffering. What cannot

[5] Pope John Paul II, *On the Christian Meaning of Human Suffering* #2.
[6] Thérèse of Lisieux, 'Epilogue,' in *Story of a Soul*, p. 264.

easily be remedied on the global scale can sometimes be soothed in the particular body-person. Among affluent nations, 'suffering' has gradually been expanded in meaning to encompass discomfort, monotony, embarrassment, or limitation. Many instances of these can be overcome, but when suffering has no ready-to-hand alleviation, as is the case with terminal illness, physical incapacity associated with aging, or accidental injury, it may seem to those without belief in a provident God that the only solution is *to eliminate the sufferer*. A Theology of the Body applicable to the present age must take into account the gamut of contemporary experience and conviction regarding suffering. Lorenzo Albecete points to the communal dimensions of suffering, saying that the reality of human suffering is to be met in terms of co-suffering with Christ:

> Redemption does not eliminate suffering. I repeat again – to eliminate suffering, to wipe it out by our own human means, is an injustice. It is to act unjustly toward the human person. Not even the mystery of redemption will eliminate it. It changes its meaning from an occasion of diminishment to an occasion of the affirmation of one's unsurpassable dignity, of Jesus Himself and the glory of God who is Love, a love stronger than sin and death.[7]

'We carry with us in our body the death of Jesus,' said St. Paul, 'so that the life of Jesus, too, may always be seen in our body. Indeed, while we are still alive, we are consigned to our death every day, for the sake of Jesus, so that in our mortal flesh the life of Jesus, too, may be openly shown' (2 Cor. 4:10–11). The mystery of human suffering reveals the mystery of Christ.

Created in the image and likeness of God, every human being is called to image selfless love, expressing the inner relations of divine life. In that light Albacete offers the bold reflection: 'The world of suffering is the result of a tragedy that occurred when the first Adam betrayed his identity under the suggestions of the Great Deceiver.' For that reason, the link between the first Adam and the second, Christ, cannot be broken: '*Otherwise*, it would mean to break the Trinity apart.'[8]

[7] Lorenzo Albacete, 'The Relief of Suffering,' Lecture 5, McGivney Lectures (Washington, D.C., Summer, 1991). Audio-tape: John Paul II Institute for Studies on Marriage and Family, Washington, D.C.
[8] Lorenzo Albacete, 'The Relief of Suffering,' Lecture 5.

What this means is that the dignity of both suffering and sufferer resides ultimately in the selfless love of trinitarian Persons, and its corporeal expression in the Incarnate Jesus Christ. When Peter advised Jesus not to speak of his coming suffering, he was quickly told that he was thinking in satanic terms, striking at the core of Jesus' mission (see Matt. 16:21–23).

To deny the meaning of suffering, to consider it unworthy of humanity, is to diminish an understanding of the trinitarian mystery, the divine communion of Persons forever given in mutual Self-gift that is redemptively extended to humanity in Jesus Christ through his Incarnation and redemptive Self-offering. The incalculable worth and dignity of every human life, and the capacity to share in redemptive Self-gift derives from each person's vocation to be image of trinitarian love and life.[9] At the Last Supper, Jesus prayed for indwelling union with those gathered at the paschal meal: 'Holy Father, keep those you have given me true to your name, so that they may be one like us.... Father, may they be one in us, as you are in me and I am in you' (Jn. 17:11, 21). Earlier in the Last Discourse, Jesus had told them that they would know weeping and wailing, but their sorrow, like that of a woman prior to childbirth, would give way to joy because it was life-giving (see Jn. 16:20–22). Love requires suffering, and there is no greater love than to lay down one's life for another (see Jn. 15:13). Certain sufferings such as illness, anxiety, and bereavement have a commonality in the human family. Revelation and Tradition interpret them as concrete occasions for encountering God either directly or through one another. This does not mean that the sufferer maintains a composed clarity, or that the mystery of suffering is completely explicable. The *Catechism of the Catholic Church* states that the world of daily experience can seem distant from the one promised by faith. Evil, suffering, injustice and death seem 'to contradict the Good News,' shaking faith and becoming temptations.[10] The amazement of those who heard Jesus' description of the Last Judgment (see Matt. 28) indicates the human difficulty in perceiving the meaning of varied forms of suffering. His promise to reward anyone who has given a drink

[9] See development concerning inner life of the Trinity and the meaning of this mystery for humanity in Sister M. Timothy Prokes, *Mutuality*.
[10] See *Catechism of the Catholic Church*, #164. See also #309, #1502, and #1006.

of cold water in his name also indicates the significance of ordinary suffering.

In the basic nuptial meaning of embodiment, every person is created in God's image to be a *gift*, given and received.[11] Whatever is judged to be useless or repugnant (or something to be escaped or destroyed 'by right') cannot be offered or received as gift. It is at this depth that the seriousness of suffering is to be understood. This does not mean that persons of faith do not experience fear, even dread, in face of suffering. The example of Jesus in Gethsemane is revelatory in that regard. Although he sweat blood in assuming to himself all the sufferings of humanity, he did not escape 'his hour,' nor revile those who particularized his own passion. He transformed his own, and all human suffering, by making it a perfect expression of saving love, in and through his body.

ILLNESS, AGING, AND THE CALL TO COMPLETION

A major theme of Luke's Gospel is Jesus' 'going up to Jerusalem,' the place that would mark the completion of his earthly mission. There, at the proper time, he would meet what the Gospel describes as 'his hour.' He would neither be deterred from completing his earthly mission in that place, nor be hastened into those culminating moments before the 'hour' had come. The reflections of the early Church indicate that a certain fullness of time was needed for the conception of Jesus, as well as for his Paschal suffering and death. The Old Covenant writer, Ecclesiastes, poetically stated the enduring insight: there is a season and a time for everything.

The present age, so gifted with technological short-cuts, is impatient with waiting for the 'fullness of time.' The innate rhythms of bodily life on both human and non-human levels, can be frustrating and the tendency is to either hurry or forestall events, according to individual advantage and/or taste. Even

---

[11] In my previous book, *Mutuality: The Human Image of Divine Love*, I have suggested that *the ontological basis of ALL reality is gift*, deriving from the Creator who brought forth all creation from nothing, as gift.

vegetables are coaxed into yielding fruit in concentrated periods of time through the elimination of natural cycles of light and darkness. Certain animals are confined in cramped quarters and treated as machines to produce large quantities of milk and meat in a short duration of time. The loss of respect for innate rhythms and the mysterious meaning of 'fullness of time' can lead to cruelty. The imposition of suffering on lesser forms of life is also manifest in the treatment of persons.

For decades, human life has been manipulated at its inception. This has become so 'ordinary' that there is little or no hesitation in commercial dealings involving sperm, ova, and fertility hormones in order to produce specialty children, tailored to suit their sponsors' desires. Parallel to this are the instruments and processes that eliminate those considered undesirable. If a child will bring 'suffering' to those who have participated in its conception, there is a widespread conviction that it should not live: suffering is to be eliminated from the lives of those who want to 'have' a desirable child, or those who wish to dispose of an unwanted child. In a similar vein, it is asserted that the conclusion of life can be controlled according to individual and group desires, in order to obviate suffering. The euphemistic language employed to describe such decisions shows a departure from responsibility within a trinitarian, redemptive understanding of life and the body-person as gifts, given in trust and called to be brought to completion in relationship. Euthanists, for example, speak of suicide as 'self-deliverance.' They contest that taking a life (either that of a child in the womb, or one's own life at a moment of choice) is a 'right' to be respected according to individual choice and supported by technical and personal expertise. What formerly would have been recognized as murder can now selectively be termed a 'medical procedure.'

Aging is not simply a descent into oblivion. It is a going where one has not been before, a participation in the mystery that Jesus drew to Peter's attention. When you are old, he told him, others will fasten a belt around your waist and take you where you would rather not go (see Jn. 21:18). The loss of physical dexterity and mental agility signals a bringing to completion what has often been obscured by frantic activity. Both Old and New Testaments address the work that God brings to completion, indeed can *only* bring to completion as the fullest realization of life, in certain women and men in their late mature years. Abraham and Sarah, at the fountainhead of the faith, are exemplary in that regard. The Letter to the Hebrews (11:8–19) includes a reflection on Abraham and Sarah who because of their faith were made fruitful in their advanced years. Of Abraham it is said: 'There came from one man, and one who was already as good as dead himself,' uncountable descendants, equal to the number of stars or grains of sand on the seashore. Hannah and Elizabeth also conceived children of destiny in their advanced years. Had they decided to terminate their own lives in difficult times, they would have annihilated their unique missions, obviated their co-creative vocation in union with the ultimate source of life of whom Isaiah wrote: 'My thoughts are not your thoughts, my ways not your ways – it is Yahweh who speaks' (Is. 55:8)

Psychologist Erik Erikson specified eight major stages in the development of a long life. He called the two final stages 'adulthood' and 'mature adulthood,' citing the predominant qualities of each together with their characteristic virtues and vices. Adulthood, he maintained, was a time of either generativity or stagnation. The generative person sees beyond his/her own generation with its vision and interests, showing care and nurturance for both those who are older and younger. If an adult stagnates, there is self-absorption and the tendency to treat *self* as one's child, nurturing self rather than the next generation. This stage, said Erikson, will be characterized either by integrity or despair and disgust. A generative life brings comradeship with preceding generations. Commenting on Erikson's work, Donald Capps says that the mature person of integrity will accept life for what it is, including the persons who have been significant in one's personal history. They will not simply be concerned for their own identity, but will take responsibility for life, being capable of emotional integration with the image-bearers of the past, transcending the limits of their own life cycle.[12]

The habits formed through a lifetime and the attitudes that a person has in regard to their embodiment are crucial in dealing with the corporeal events that transpire in the aging process. What we have seen regarding acceptance of bodily limitations,

---

[12] See Donald Capps, *Life Cycle Theory and Pastoral Care* (Philadelphia, 1983), p. 29.

the meaning of work, and above all, the basic meaning of the body as nuptial will all come to a focus in terms of coming to a faith understanding of each phase of life.

Scripture describes how those entrusted with a mission experience a sense of inadequacy and realize that their mission is for the benefit of the whole people, not for personal aggrandizement. They also have an assurance that God will be present with them, enabling the fulfillment of the mission. Without that faith context, suffering and difficulty seem unsurmountable – meaningless obstacles from which, in Derek Humphrey's words, one seeks a 'Final Exit.' The beginnings and endings of human life are immersed in divine mystery, each an aspect of the total *gift* of life. These moments signal the notion of gift in a particular manner when received without manipulation. Wisdom is the virtue of mature adulthood, said Erikson. It signifies a detached concern with life in the face of death itself. The person of wisdom can relinquish without turning against, can know sadness without attacking the object of its sadness. When the acuity of the senses diminishes, and the vigor of physical activity subsides, the experience of loss can evoke a preparedness for transcending transformation, or it can bring about a world-weariness accompanied by resentment and self-contempt.[13] To seize a gift or demand it on one's own terms is a defiance of the meaning of gift.

Illness, impairment, and the decline of familiar powers mark the body in a particular manner, but they are never simply physical realities: they permeate the entire person and indicate a time of transformation. Suffering is transformative of the entire body-person. It frequently requires one to draw back from feverish activity, and wait upon what is beyond one's control or manipulation. In *The Pregnant Virgin*, Marion Woodman recounts a childhood experience. When she was three years old, her father who was an excellent gardener, brought a branch into the kitchen. To her child's eye, it seemed to have a small 'lump' attached to it. Pinning the branch on a curtain, her father said that a caterpillar had made a chrysalis for itself within the unsightly lump and that one day it would emerge as a butterfly. She tells of eyeing the dull lump with disbelief each morning as she ate her cereal. Her father had cautioned her to be patient: it

[13] See Donald Capps, *Life Cycle Theory*, pp. 47–48.

only looked dead, he said, but remarkable changes were taking place inside. The transformation was difficult work – nothing else could be accomplished while transformation occurred within the protective shell. One morning, says Woodman, she sensed that she was not alone in the kitchen and she saw a 'shimmering translucent light' near the empty chrysalis. It was her first encounter with death and rebirth.[14]

What is the human body's significance in death? What occurs to its nuptial meaning? Theology of the Body tends always toward that ultimate meaning of embodiment.

[14] See Marion Woodman, *The Pregnant Virgin: A Process of Psychological Transformation* (Toronto, 1985), pp. 13–14.

12

Bodily Death and Resurrection

H UMAN death implicates the whole body-person. While death
is one of the most familiar certainties of human existence, it
is simultaneously the horizon which separates ordinary,
acquired, experiential knowledge from that which can only be
interpreted through the gift of divine Revelation. In Christian
faith, the mystery of human death is a participation in Christ's
death and resurrection. In both of the Creeds prayed in the
liturgy, there is, together with the profession of belief in Christ's
death and resurrection, an affirmation of belief in 'the resurrection of the body, and life everlasting' (Apostles' Creed) – or as the
Nicene Creed states it: 'We expect the resurrection of the dead
and the life of the world to come.'

The mystery of bodily death can be reflected upon from several
perspectives: 1) the phenomena available to ordinary knowledge;
2) the boundary point that constitutes death: a mystery of continuity and transformation; 3) Christ's redemptive bodily death
and resurrection; and 4) Mary's Assumption and its implications
for those who die in Christ.

DEATH PHENOMENA

Death is ever-present in human experience. In the aftermath of
the twentieth century's two world wars, the 'developed nations'
of the West seemed for a time to enter a period of denial regarding death, cloaking its actuality and finality. Evelyn Waugh's
novel, *The Beloved*, satirized attempts to sentimentalize and/or
deny death. In the waning years of the twentieth century, however, images of death in the visual media make it visually immediate and familiar. The assassination of President John F. Kennedy
in 1963 proved a turning point. Into a death-denying society
there was suddenly thrust the immediacy and reality of death.

159

The image of an international leader shattered in the presence of spectators has been etched on the common memory. In ensuing decades, what was once considered taboo, that from which one shielded children's eyes, streams into the intimate circumstances of daily life. In a manner similar to that which has been noted above regarding overt *sexual* activity, previous reticence to open discussion of death has given way to a media-saturation of images and accounts dealing with it. 'Chosen death' is now perceived as a right to be pursued and a choice to be made available upon request.

In summarizing contemporary attitudes toward abortion and all forms of violence, Pope John Paul II has spoken of the 'culture of death' that characterizes the present age. The collective horror that followed the exposure of European death camps in the first half of this century has yielded to an ambivalence about death. Two factors underlie these changed attitudes toward death and the phenomena that characterize it: 1) loss of belief in God and transcendent life after death; and 2) the conviction that individual choice and self-determination are the ultimate meaning of human existence. Sherwin Nuland, teacher of surgery and the history of medicine at Yale University, observes:

> Much less commonly than at any other time in this millennium do the dying nowadays turn to God and the promise of an afterlife when the present life is fading. . . . These days, many hospitalized patients die only when a doctor has decided that the right time has come. Beyond the curiosity and the problem-solving challenge fundamental to good research, I believe that the fantasy of controlling nature lies at the very basis of modern science.[1]

Loss, pain, helplessness, loneliness, separation and abandonment have always been associated with death, and each has a corporeal basis. But there is a new impatience with those mental and emotional crises that denote loss of control over life and death. A new form of denial has replaced former reactions to death – a denial characterized by practical attempts to manage death and deny the vulnerabilities associated with it. There is the desire to be capable of forestalling it, or of summoning it at the

[1] Sherwin B. Nuland, *How We Die: Reflections on Life's Final Chapter* (New York, 1994), pp. 256, 259.

moment of personal choice. In the phrase of Derek Humphrey of the Hemlock Society, death becomes 'self-deliverance.'

DEATH: TRANSFORMATION AND CONTINUITY

Within the context of resurrection, death is the transition of the whole body-person from a space-time milieu to eternal life. Material elements that formerly expressed a unified outward expression of the entire body-person no longer function personally. The coordinated organs of the body rapidly deteriorate when the unitive flow of oxygen and blood ceases. Although the familiar contours of the lived body endure, death brings a disintegration among the elements that formed the 'I-body.'

Replying to members of the early Church in Corinth, who had queried him concerning the resurrected body, St. Paul wrote: 'Someone may ask, "How are dead people raised, and what sort of body do they have when they come back?" These are stupid questions' (1 Cor. 15:35–36). Despite his blunt assessment of their questions, Paul used the analogy of *good seed* to assist them in pondering the mystery of the resurrected body. What is sown as good seed in the ground must die in order that new life may emerge.[2] He pointed out that God has provided an appropriate body for everything. Each kind of seed receives its unique kind of God-given body, but *what emerges from the earth will not resemble what was sown* (just as the butterfly's body does not resemble the caterpillar that has been encompassed in a cocoon). The

[2] The ancient dictum that the blood of martyrs is the seed of Christians continues to be a meaningful image. For example, in the crypt chapel of Maria Regina Martyrum in West Berlin, established as a memorial to the martyrs and confessors whose lives were lost in the Nazi regime, there are three graves. The central one holds a document telling the 'Martyrology' of those who died for freedom of religion and conscience, but whose bodies were either denied burial or discarded in unmarked graves. Father Alfred Delp, SJ, who died on the gallows of Plotzensee, close to the memorial church, wrote in one of his last letters: 'After one thing I strive: to sink into God's earth and into His hand as a fertile, healthy seed.' When he died, February 2, 1945, 'his ashes were scattered over the fields. Hitler wanted it as a sign of complete annihilation. But was it not a symbol? These martyrs became the seed of our people's new hope. Because of the new hope many people pray at the graves of this crypt.' *Maria Regina Martyrum*, trans. Raimund Grieger (Berlin, 1965), p. 29.

death of a seed is not an obstacle to its continuity, but the necessary condition for its passage into new life. It is the same for the resurrection of those who have died, said Paul:

> The thing that is sown is perishable but what is raised is imperishable; the thing that is sown is contemptible but what is raised is glorious; the thing that is sown is weak but what is raised is powerful; when it is sown it embodies the soul, when it is raised it embodies the spirit (1 Cor. 15:42–44).

Paul used the term *psychikon* to indicate the earthly, physical body, and *pneumatikon* to indicate the spiritual, risen body. In the understanding of his time, *psyche* meant that which makes the body live and could refer to that which makes animals live. It could also mean the living person or that which gave natural life to the body. The *pneuma*, on the other hand, meant that gift of the Spirit by which human life is divinized – a process completed after death. While Greek philosophers thought that the *nous* (or 'soul') of the person escaped the body at death in order to survive immortally, 'Christians thought of immortality more in terms of the restoration of the whole person, involving a resurrection of the body effected by the Spirit or divine principle which God withdrew from human beings because of sins, Gn 6:3, but restored to all who are united to the risen Christ'[3] who is life-giving Spirit. The pneumatic body is incorruptible and immortal and is no longer subject to the laws of space and time, so its description cannot be found in reference to ordinary matter. The phenomena apparent just prior to death no longer suffice for explaining the characteristics of a resurrected body.

The boundary point that *constitutes* death is the interface between time and eternity. We have already seen that the body's meaning is nuptial. Within the mystery of its existence, and concomitant with the human vocation to come into a communion of persons, the living body itself is a 'wedding' of matter and spirit, of personal identity and the elements of the material universe. Made in the image of the triune God, each person's body is his/her Real Symbol, destined for a union that can only be fully realized in eternal life. In death, the body becomes the wedding site of earthly and eternal life. The death of saints is

---

[3] *The Jerusalem Bible*, f.n. 'L', p. 309 (NT).

described as their *transitus* day, their day of transition from the limitations of earthly life to inseparable union with God and with all who are in the Communion of Saints.

All that has earlier been stated concerning the body as *gift* must be recalled here. It is only in the context of salvific gift that the difficult splendor of death can be realized. Within that context, death unites two seemingly incongruous factors: *continuity* and *transformation*. As Paul notes in 1 Corinthians, death requires a letting-go of one way of being body-person in order to be expressed anew in a transcendent manner. There is, however, a continuity: *the identity of the person remains.* When 'Saul' was thrown to the ground on his journey to Damascus, it was not a delegate of Jesus who spoke to him. The Living One who addressed him was the Risen Christ, the One who had died and had risen irrevocably. Later St. Paul would tell the Corinthians that what he taught he had himself received, learned: that Christ died for our sins; that he had indeed been buried; that he had risen to life; and that he had appeared to witnesses, Paul himself being the last (see 1 Cor. 15:3–8).

It is the *body* that signs the transition: the Real Symbol of the person indicates that a *transitus* has occurred from time/space existence to eternal life. No matter what the circumstances of an individual person's death, whether it comes swiftly or after protracted illness, there is immense dignity in the passage. What happens to the whole body-person at the moment of death is of inexhaustible theological concern.

Ladislaus Boros has advanced a theoretical interpretation of what he terms the 'in-death moment.' All life tends toward that moment as enabling a person's first totally integral human act. We are so much more than our individual acts, he says. Rather, they well up from an incomparable abundance so that in every act of knowing, willing, remembering and creating there is an experience of incompleteness, together with a longing for totality. In regard to the will, for example, there is a radical lack of restraint: a person always aims beyond the immediate content of any specific act of willing. At the heart of human volition is the urge for *more*, an urge that can never be totally fulfilled in our present manner of being. It is characteristic of our existence, says Boros, that there is a never-reduced inequality between this urge for *all* and what we specifically will at any given moment.

At the source of human activity there is a mysterious 'unknown' that ever eludes our grasp, making it impossible to abide in total contentment. Augustine voiced this memorably: 'Our hearts are restless until they rest in thee!' Reflection on ordinary experience confirms this. Children have the illusion that the acquisition of a certain toy or the arrival of Christmas will bring a sense of complete fulfillment. When these are actualized, however, they result not only in joy and a certain satisfaction, but also in the evocation of new and more intensified longings. This kind of self-illusion recurs throughout life: the concept that *more* (whatever its specific expression) will slake insatiable thirst. The child's volitional desires grow into adult status: it seems that inner depth restlessness will be quelled by a marriage, accomplishments, wealth or power. Boros says that there is a 'never-reduced inadequation' between our *urge* and what we actually will: it is a 'distinguishing mark of our existence':

> Man, after all, can only find rest when the will for the determinate object is capable of absorbing completely the full intensity of the will's elemental drive. . . . Every time a man wishes to establish his lasting home in one spot, the thrust of his own being bears him on to fresh spaces. . . . the will has never willed itself completely and to the full.[4]

What is true of our willing is also true of our knowing, remembering, sensing and creating. There is a transcendence in each act that cannot attain perfect fulfillment now. It is evident that the human person is really pressing on 'in an unordered manner towards a decision in which, when he has at last become one with his whole volition, he may be able to take his stand face to face with God.'[5] Thus, in every human action *God* is the inescapable factor, whether one is capable of adverting to that, or not.

Only in the 'in-death moment' is the human person capable for the first time of achieving full volition. What has been embryonic prior to death is brought into a fully unified effectiveness. All earthly life is a preparation for that moment. Only in death will all that has previously been fragmentary and revisable come together, says Boros: a person's volition will achieve full union with itself by freely accepting or rejecting everything for which it

[4] Ladislaus Boros, *The Mystery of Death* (New York, 1965), pp. 26, 27.
[5] Ladislaus Boros, *The Mystery of Death*, p. 28.

has been striving, right from the beginning.[6] The 'in-death moment' is the first possibility of a total human choice. All distractions and tentative decisions will give way to a first complete, unified act of the whole person.

By way of contrast, Boros' analysis of the 'in-death moment' illumines the late-twentieth century assertion of individual choice as the ultimate value in human existence. Cut off from a divine and eternal meaning, the insistent longing of a person to make a free, total choice can lead to the conviction that human volition has been perfectly fulfilled when a *specific, limited choice* has overcome all external opposition. The more serious the focus of choice (such as those regarding life and death decisions) the more it may *seem* that the capacity to come to a total, human act has been fulfilled. The reality postulated by Boros is much more profound, however.

The 'in-death moment' (not the moment just prior to actual death) brings the first capability of making such a full, personal act. There is no altering of a person's complete act of will at this point because it *is* the whole person in total choice. If human existence were of unending temporariness and incompletion, says Boros, it would be the devastation of freedom. We would go mad if we could never die because we are called to total capacity (and here it must be recalled that the ultimate human capacity is to be self-gift in a communion of persons). We strive toward a final decision 'where all inconstancy and reversibility are overcome in a free positing of ultimate finality.'[7] It is the whole body-person that undergoes the transition moment of death. The Roman Catholic Church affirms both 1) the natural immortality of the human soul, and 2) the resurrection of the body. The total choice made in death affects the entire body-person. Whatever the appearance of the resurrected body, it will express the identity of the individual person. Resurrection will not involve the annihilation of individual identity, nor will individuality be expressed in the immortal soul only – but in the resurrected, embodied person.

That is a fundamental reason why it is impossible to reconcile belief in reincarnation with a Christian understanding of body-

---

[6] See Ladislaus Boros, *The Mystery of Death*, p. 30.
[7] Ladislaus Boros, *The Mystery of Death*, p. 95.

person. According to reincarnational theory, the real identity of a human being resides only in the spiritual aspect. Depending upon the amount of positive *karma* at death, an individual may be thrust back to earth repeatedly in either a 'higher' or 'lower' state of material embodiment until perfection is achieved. This would mean that the body is sub-personal and interchangeable, serving as a housing or clothing of the real 'I'. In theories of reincarnation, the body is perceived to be discarded at death while an enduring spiritual reality is plunged into another material configuration. In the Christian understanding of body-person, however, there is esteem for the unique body-meaning of each person, a meaning brought to fullest expression in Jesus Christ.

CHRIST'S REDEMPTIVE DEATH AND RESURRECTION

Christians profess that the Risen Christ continues to be effectively present. Cipriano Vaggagini, asserting that Christ's physical body has an eternal, active and permanent function, says that clear perceptions regarding Christ's resurrection (and our own) and the Eucharist require a realization of 'the ever active and permanent part willed by God that is played by the physical body of Christ in the accomplishment of salvation in us.'[8]

The bodily resurrection of Christ is foundational for Christian anthropology. The Risen Christ is bodily present within history – but not in the same material manner as that which characterized it prior to his death and resurrection. In the terminology of Christian tradition, Christ's risen body is *agile* (that is, not bound by limitations of space and time) and *impassible* (that is, incapable of earthly suffering). Possessed by and totally docile to the Holy Spirit, Christ, in love for the Father, offers his risen body as total, permanent gift to the Church, his bride. His risen body expresses the timeless and permanent Paschal gift of self most particularly in the Eucharist. St. Paul deftly summarizes how bodily resurrection is at the heart of apostolic preaching: if the dead do not rise, then Christ did not rise. But if Christ did not

---

[8] Cipriano Vaggagini, *The Flesh*, p. 16.

rise, there is no redemption; we are still in our sins and faith in Christ is futile (see 1 Cor. 15:14–19). If Christ has not risen, said Paul, self-sacrificing Christians would be the most pathetic of all people and those who swore to the truth of his resurrection would be liars. *It is Christ's resurrection that establishes the bodily resurrection of those incorporated with him in Baptism.*

Everything that Jesus lived out in his earthly mission was in terms of relationship, fulfilling what was essential to divine and human relationships. In confronting human death, he did not take advantage of divine power to evade it. He awaited the time appointed by the Father, in the Spirit. He did not stipulate how much pain he would endure, nor did he demand to be released from severe physical suffering and humiliation. His intimate prayer was 'My Father . . . if it is possible, let this cup pass me by. Nevertheless, let it be as you, not I, would have it' (Matt. 26:39). His prayer expressed keen realization of the horrors to be endured, together with a *fiat* to all that would be required in accepting death. He took upon himself a wholly human death, becoming one with all who undergo even the most painful transitions into eternal life.

While the resurrection is the *sine quo non* of Christian faith, it is the manner in which it is interpreted that is crucial. Attitudes toward the human body directly affect understanding of this most critical turning point in Christian faith. Raymond Brown designates several differing interpretations of Christ's resurrection among 'believing theologians.' He distinguishes 1) those who think that the body of Jesus *did* decompose; 2) those who want to affirm simply 'Jesus lives' while bypassing the real question of bodily resurrection; 3) those who are agnostic, or uncertain about the corruption of Jesus' body in the tomb, and prefer to use 'exaltation phrases' that avoid the issue; and finally 4) those who hold that Jesus was transformed beyond the limits of space and time, and who affirm that he will not die again.[9] It is the last of these four positions that accords with official Roman Catholic doctrine and which clarifies the necessary distinction between resurrection and resuscitation. In this interpretation, Jesus did not have a 'near-death experience,' nor was he revived

---

[9] See Raymond Brown, *The Virginal Conception and Bodily Resurrection of Jesus* (New York, 1973), pp. 69–78.

after what today would be termed 'being pronounced clinically dead.' In his own ministering to others, Jesus restored to a widowed mother the young man who was being carried to his burial. He raised the daughter of Jairus from her deathbed and indicated that she had need of ordinary food. He summoned his friend Lazarus from the tomb four days after his burial: it is significant that Lazarus reclined at table with him the following week, much to the chagrin of his enemies (see Jn. 12:9–11). In each of these cases, the person was restored to ordinary, embodied space-time life.

Jesus' resurrection, however, is radically different. His real and complete humanity was transformed in a transcendent manner, no longer subject to space/time conditions and the eventual need to die again. His resurrection constitutes an eschatological event – already belonging to the 'end times.' Our language concerning it can only be analogous, as St. Paul's was. History and eschatology *do* touch, but death is always a confronting of the mysterious transition point at the horizon of human comprehension.

IMPLICATIONS OF MARY'S ASSUMPTION

In 1950, a half decade after World War Two, when humanity was forever marked by the Holocaust in Europe and the nuclear devastation of Hiroshima and Nagasaki, Pope Pius XII defined as a divinely revealed truth 'that the Immaculate Mother of God, the ever Virgin Mary, the course of her earthly life having been completed, was assumed body and soul into heavenly glory.'[10] Throughout the history of the Church, divinely revealed truths have been brought to formal dogmatic definition when there was explicit need for their confirmation. At other times dogmatic definitions have corrected explicit errors.

The definition of Mary's Assumption into glory as a total embodied human person came at a particularly apt moment. The first half of the twentieth century had opened the secrets of matter in a dramatic manner – but these secrets had been exploited through unparalleled devastation of bodies and the material universe. Moreover, human consciousness had been dimmed

[10] Pope Pius XII, 'Munificentissimus Deus,' in *Acta Apostolica Sedis*, 42 (November 4, 1950), p. 770.

regarding the eternal destiny of the whole person, body and spirit. The simple core of the dogmatic statement concerning Mary's Assumption affirms the relational, enduring meaning of the body-person, emphasizing that the body's meaning does not cease in death. In earlier chapters it has been seen how Pope John Paul II has theologically and anthropologically explored human origins in Genesis, repeatedly naming the body's meaning as nuptial. Just as the meaning of embodiment illumines prayer, communication, work, sexuality, illness and suffering, so too does it elucidate the 'in-death moment' and the eschatological destiny of each person. John Paul II reflects:

> In fact, in the whole perspective of his own 'history,' man will not fail to confer a nuptial meaning on his own body. Even if this meaning undergoes and will undergo many distortions, it will always remain the deepest level, which demands to be revealed in all its simplicity and purity, and to be shown in its whole truth, as a sign of the 'image of God.' The way that goes from the mystery of creation to the 'redemption of the body' (cf. Rom. 8) also passes here.[11]

How can the nuptial or unitive meaning of the body-person be maintained and actually come to its fullest possibility in and beyond death? Writing of Christ's resurrection, Karl Rahner stressed that it is *our* flesh which he took up and glorified. Christians, from the beginning, have held that 'eternal glory is even now a possibility in the history of the world, this humanity and this flesh; already a possibility because in the flesh of Christ, which is a part of the world, it is already a reality.'[12] What the Assumption dogma unequivocally means is that Mary, as simply human (not like her Son, a hypostatic unity of the divine and human) has attained the complete realization of her humanity, body and soul, in glory. Following so closely on the formerly unthinkable degradations of the human body and the material universe that had taken place in the first half of the twentieth century, the dogmatic declaration confirmed as a revealed truth Mary's bodily Assumption, and decisively affirmed the dignity of human life. Death is not the opportunistic annihilation of enemies, ridding them permanently from one's presence; nor is it

---

[11] Pope John Paul II, *Original Unity of Man and Woman*, p. 118.
[12] Karl Rahner, *Mary, Mother of the Lord* (New York, 1963), p. 89.

a) a favored option for asserting personal choice or b) the permanent escape hatch in the face of pain, helplessness and humiliation. In faith, death is confessed as the possibility of entrance into the eternal wedding feast. It implies the donation of one's entire self in love, a 'letting go' with nothing withheld, in order to be received into the communion of divine Persons in whom all other relationships find their source. The possibility of choice is real. When the recently restored 'Last Judgment' fresco of Michelangelo was unveiled, Pope John Paul II made particular reference to the artist's depiction of more than 300 figures awaiting judgment, praising the portrayal of 'the integral beauty of the body.' The work speaks the truths of faith from every corner, said John Paul: 'Above all we are faced with the glory of Christ's humanity. He will truly come in his humanity to judge the living and the dead, penetrating to the depths of human consciences and revealing the power of his redemption.'[13]

In a nuptial understanding of embodiment, the beginning and ending of earthly human life are located within the mystery of love and relationship. These are realities not to be 'grasped at,' or technologically maneuvered. A wedding of spirit and matter, the living body bears a personal, conscious and unconscious relational history. The destinies of other persons and the cosmos itself are influenced by every conception and every death.

When the unfathomable energy within even minute elements of matter was released in the twentieth century, *contemporary humanity began to experience a radical inability to contain and release the potential of matter without becoming destructive. The focus of this inability has moved from the arena of external weaponry to the internal forum – to sexual energy, and to creative energies that are expressed in the technological manipulation of embodied persons.* As I have written previously, the explosive release of atomic energy has irrevocably changed our ways of understanding body and matter-energy exchange. The custom-made wineskins that formerly contained our ways of treating bodies and matter have split, but our experimental ways of trying to hold the release of energy are still primitive and dangerous. 'It is not the release of energy, nor the marvelous

---

[13] Cited in 'Fresco Reveals the "Integral Beauty of the Body",' in *Prairie Messenger*, St. Peter's Abbey, Muenster, Saskatchewan, April 25, 1994, p. 20.

interplay of matter and energy that are troublesome, but our present incapacity to hold this process into life-giving potential without simultaneously causing destruction. The human body – microcosm of earth's elemental, vegetative and animal life brought to consciousness – participates in that capacity for creative interchange and energy release. *When the atom was released into new possibility, the human body also entered a new phase of existence on earth.*[14] Theology of the Body does not further the illusion that this highly desirable release into new possibility comes through isolated, individualized choices without reference to the Creator, the human community's shared stewardship, and all that transcends the present era of history.

ASSUMPTION: TRANSFORMATION, NOT DESTRUCTION

Mary's Assumption into glory, body and soul, in light of Christ's redemptive death and resurrection, is also a participation in those qualities which characterize his resurrection: continuity and transformation. Mary retains her identity. What is particularly significant for a Theology of the Body is the faith-based principle that *already* within the present history of the universe, strictly human life has been taken up *totally* into eternal glory. Mary has attained fullness of perfection as an embodied person. In promulgating the Assumption dogma, Pope Pius XII recalled how Bonaventure, writing in the Middle Ages, had said that Mary's blessedness would not be complete if she were not glorified as a whole person: the soul by itself is not the person. Just as the glorified body of Christ expressed his history in ways that not only puzzled his immediate followers, but also allowed them to recognize him, so, too, Mary's glorified presence manifests her historical journey. In this regard, Karl Rahner has observed:

> What is glorified retains a real connexion with the unglorified world ... an occurrence of glorification possesses objectively its determinate place in this world's time, even if this point in time marks precisely the point at which a portion of this world ceases

[14] Sister M. Timothy Prokes, 'The Nuptial Meaning of Body in Light of Mary's Assumption,' *Communio*, X, 2 (Summer, 1984), pp. 162–163.

to endure time itself, in so far as it is different from all others while remaining in unity with the whole.[15]

The privileges celebrated in Mary are grounded in her body. The doctrine of her Immaculate Conception refers to her freedom from original sin from the beginning of her existence in her mother's womb. It has been defined as dogma that at her life's conclusion, she was bodily assumed into glory. Since Mary's body-person was never given to sin, and since human persons are destined for eternal life, her Assumption underscores the question: *what would transformation from space-time existence into eternal life be, had there been no sin?* It is clear from the above discussion concerning the possibility of a first *totally human act* in the in-death moment, that human fulfillment could never be attained through an endless existence within the limits of space and time. The longing for transcendence is inherent in the human longing for fulfillment. But, except for Mary's Assumption into glory, we do not know what transformation in death would be if human persons had not sinned.

Daily life is characterized by countless forms of transformation. Earthly life already bears the transformative principle within it. In some ways, Mary's Assumption should be one of the most familiar dogmas of Christian faith, since the analogies within lived experience are constantly with us. Each time we eat and drink, each time we experience breathing, digestion and elimination we *live* the mystery of continuity in transformation. Neither Christ nor Mary were exempt from the very 'earthy' processes leading to death and transcendence into glory. The earthly life of the God-man and that of his totally human Mother reveal the immense dignity of ordinary daily existence. They also reveal that, despite the goodness of life in a space-time universe, there is an irreversible advance toward eternal life, with the *meaning* of that transcendent movement anchored in relationships both divine and human.

Both the resurrection of Christ and the Assumption of Mary indicate that death does not mean an alienation from the material universe. Rather, they indicate a more profound way of relating to created matter. The Eucharist is Christ's personal gift in the

---

[15] Karl Rahner, 'The Interpretation of the Dogma of the Assumption,' in *Theological Investigations I*, trans. Cornelius Ernst (Baltimore, 1961), p. 224.

resurrected body and blood. Christians pray to the Mother of God as one who, in glory, retains her identity and is recognized as woman, virgin and mother – not simply a disembodied spirit. Mary's Assumption points to the enduring significance of her own body, but it also confirms the dignity of every human body. From the early age of the martyrs to the present time, this dignity has been recognized in the care of the often-mutilated bodies of those who have been maimed and/or killed for their fidelity in professing the faith. At first, in the catacombs and secret burial places, and later on the altars of Christian churches throughout the world, the Eucharist has been offered over the 'first class relics' of the saints. What has formed part of their Real Symbol is forever precious. Matter is the bonding point between glorified and still unglorified matter. It is the sacramental locus for relationships in the Communion of Saints.

Every sacrament requires bodily presence. In the administering of four sacraments, the body of the recipient is anointed with blessed oil. In the sacraments, water, candles, bread and wine, and symbolic articles of clothing are integrated with the spoken word to sign in body-centered media what is being effected on behalf of the entire person. In death, the elements that formed the living body are reverently prepared for burial, brought near the altar, blessed and incensed, and covered with a cloth that recalls their baptismal garment. From baptism, to the final prayers for the deceased, the body centers Christian experience.

Throughout Christian tradition, many persons of faith have experienced encounters with those who have died. When, after careful scrutiny and discernment, these visitations have been verified by ecclesial authorities, the Church officially recognizes their authenticity. Genuine 'apparitions' of Mary or other saints are analogous to the post-resurrection appearances of Christ. Just as the apostles experienced the Lord in his resurrected body in a manner in which the glorified *can* appear to the unglorified, so, too, those who are visited by saints experience them in terms of continuity and transformation – there is recognition of identity together with a realization of a transformed manner of presence.

Questions persist. Does this mean that other saints besides Mary are already embodied in glory? For those who have died in total loving self-gift, could final glorification have already occurred? Does Mary's Assumption exclude the possibility that others have completed the fulfillment of their body-persons? If the total body-person dies, is there an interim matter-spirit separation, or is there already a completely transformed matter-spirit union? Is it more suitable in the divine plan that all, except Christ and Mary, await the ultimate consummation of the cosmos before participating in a universal transformation?

George Shea notes that the dogmatic decree on the Assumption, *Munificentissimus Deus*, designates Mary's Immaculate Conception an *entirely* singular privilege, but it does not place such a restrictive qualification on her bodily Assumption.[16] Charles Decelles postulates that there may not be a distinction between immediate and final resurrection. For the individual person, he says, 'The two resurrections are one and the same. The "first" resurrection is the resurrection of the *soma* and so is the last.'[17] It seems that the confirmation of Mary's bodily Assumption may indicate that it is not necessarily the will of God that complete human transformation await the final consummation of the world. The doctrine of purgatory has never been understood as a space-time reality. Purgation after death, in preparation for total transformation in glory, is understood to vary greatly from individual to individual. It may be that those whose self-gift in love is total are already completely transformed in glory. Karl Rahner conjectures:

> ... salvation has already advanced so far historically that since the Resurrection it is completely 'normal' (which is not to say 'general') that there should be men in whom sin and death have already been definitively overcome.[18]

Christ's resurrection and Mary's Assumption affirm that it is a *communion of persons*, male and female (and not the God-man only) who are already taken up into glory. As both creature and redeemed, Mary signifies the possibility of ultimate glorification for all who have died in receptivity to Christ's redemptive love.

---

[16] See George W. Shea, 'The Assumption,' in *The Mystery of the Woman*, ed. Edward D. O'Connor (Notre Dame, IN, 1956), p. 76.
[17] Charles Decelles, 'A Fresh Look at the Assumption of Mary or the Idea of Resurrection Immediately After Death,' *The American Ecclesiastical Review*, 167, 3 (March, 1973), p. 159.
[18] Karl Rahner, 'The Interpretation of the Dogma of the Assumption,' p. 226.

Mary's body-person is in eternal communion with Christ. The Communion of Saints is exemplified above all in that union, confirming the dignity of both male and female. In the Christ-Mary union, the nuptial meaning of body reaches its ultimate expression.

Theology of the Body, a reflection on the meaning of embodiment and the created universe, will never be finished until the final consummation of the entire universe. This book is intended as an introduction to the most basic questions needing consideration in a Theology of the Body. It indicates the scope of the theological task which awaits 'body theologians' of the next Christian millennium.

Works Cited

Ackerman, Diane *A Natural History of the Senses* New York: Vintage Books, 1991

Albacete, Lorenzo 'The Relief of Suffering' Lecture 5 of McGivney Lecture Series, co-sponsored by John Paul II Institute and Providence Hospital, Washington, D.C., Summer, 1991

Aquinas, Thomas *Summa Theologiae* Blackfriars Latin text and English trans. New York: McGraw-Hill Book Company, 1964+

Ashley, Benedict *Theologies of the Body: Humanist and Christian* Braintree, MA: The Pope John Center, 1985

Atwood, Margaret *Surfacing* Toronto: McClelland and Stewart Limited, 1972

Balthasar, Hans Urs von *Mysterium Paschale* Aidan Nichols trans. Grand Rapids, MI: William B. Eerdmans Publishing Company, 1990

— *The Office of Peter and the Structure of the Church* Andree Emery trans. San Francisco: Ignatius Press, 1986

Barbotin, Edmond *The Humanity of Man* Matthew J. O'Connell trans. Maryknoll, NY: Orbis Books, 1975

Bell, Rudolph M. *Holy Anorexia* London: The University of Chicago Press Limited, 1985

Boff, Leonardo *Trinity and Society* Paul Burns trans. Maryknoll, NY: Orbis Books, 1988

Bone, Edith *Seven Years Solitary* London: Pan Books Limited, 1957

Booth, William 'Triumph of the Fake' *The Washington Post* (April 14, 1996): A1, A20.

Boros, Ladislaus *The Mystery of Death* New York: The Seabury Press, 1965

Bottomley, Frank *Attitudes to the Body in Western Christendom* London: Lepus Books, 1979

Brain Research and Human Consciousness Workshop (Proceedings) St. Louis, MO: Fordyce House, March 14–16, 1986

Brown, Peter *The Body in Society: Men, Women, and Sexual Renunciation in Early Christianity* New York: Columbia University Press, 1988

Brown, Raymond *The Virginal Conception and Bodily Resurrection of Jesus* New York: Paulist Press, 1973

Brungs, Robert 'Mixed Blessings: Can Ethics Determine the Middle Ground Between Science and Religion?' *Universitas*, 19, 2 (Winter, 1994): 14–17

— *You See Lights Breaking Upon Us* St. Louis, MO: Robert Brungs, 1989

— 'Hybrids, Genes and Patents,' in Institute for Theological Encounter with Science and Technology *Bulletin* (St. Louis, MO, Summer, 1995): 3–16

Capps, Donald *Life Cycle Theory and Pastoral Care* Philadelphia: Fortress Press, 1983

Capra, Fritjof, and David Steindal-Rast *Belonging to the Universe: Explorations on the Frontiers of Science and Spirituality* San Francisco: HarperCollins Publishers, 1991

Catechism of the Catholic Church Libreria Editrice Vaticana, 1994

Chardin, Pierre Teilhard de 'En quoi consiste le corps humain?' in *Science et Christ* Paris: Editions du Seuil, 1965

Congregation for the Doctrine of the Faith *Instruction on Respect for Human Life in Its Origin and on the Dignity of Procreation: Replies to Certain Questions of the Day* Vatican trans. Boston, MA: St. Paul Editions, 1987

Curran, Charles *A New Look at Christian Morality* Notre Dame IN: Fides Publishers, 1968.

— 'Encyclical Left Church Credibility Stillborn' *National Catholic Reporter* (July 16, 1993): 14–15

— *New Perspectives in Moral Theology* Notre Dame, IN: Fides Publishers, 1974

— *Themes in Fundamental Moral Theology* Notre Dame/London: University of Notre Dame Press, 1974

'Dander's Up Over "Designer Babies"' *Calgary Herald* (January 2, 1994): A2

Daube, David *The New Testament and Rabbinic Judaism* London: Athlone Press, 1965

Davis, Charles *Body as Spirit: The Nature of Religious Feeling* New York: Seabury Press, 1976.

Decelles, Charles 'A Fresh Look at the Assumption of Mary or the Idea of Resurrection Immediately After Death' *The American Ecclesiastical Review*, 167, 3 (March, 1973): 147–163

Dickinson, Robert 'Faith-Healing and Death' *Irish Biblical Studies*, 15 (June, 1993): 115–139

Dillard, Annie *Pilgrim at Tinker Creek* New York: Harper and Row Publishers, 1974

Dorsey, Larry *Space, Time and Medicine* Boulder, CO: Shambhala, 1982

Duden, Barbara 'History Beneath the Skin' CBC *IDEAS* Transcripts (Toronto, Ontario, 1991): 1–20

Ernst, Josef 'Significance of Christ's Eucharistic Body for the Unity of Church and Cosmos,' in *The Breaking of Bread* Pierre Benoit, Roland Murphy and Bastian Van Iersel eds. New York: Paulist Press, 1969: 106–116

Fletcher, Joseph 'Indicators of Humanhood: A Tentative Profile of Man' *The Hastings Center Report*, 2, 5 (November, 1972): 1–4

'Fresco Reveals the "Integral Beauty of the Body"' *Prairie Messenger* (April 25, 1994): 20

Grant, R. M. *Gnosticism and Early Christianity*, 2nd ed. New York: Columbia University Press, 1966

Green, Julien *God's Fool: The Life and Times of Francis of Assisi* Peter Heinegg trans. San Francisco: Harper and Row, 1985

Gunton, Colin E. *The Promise of Trinitarian Theology* Edinburgh: T & T Clark, 1991

Harding, Esther *Woman's Mysteries: Ancient and Modern* New York: G. P. Putnam's Sons for the C. G. Jung Foundation for Analytical Psychology, 1971

Haught, John F. 'Revelation,' in *The New Dictionary of Theology* Joseph A. Komonchak, Mary Collins and Dermot A. Lane eds. Wilmington, DE: Michael Glazier, Incorporated, 1987: 884–899

Hervieux, Jacques *The New Testament Apocrypha* New York: Hawthorn Books, 1960

Jaroff, Leon 'Iceman' *Time*, 140, 17 (October 26, 1992): 48–52

Jerusalem Bible Alexander Jones, *et al* eds. Garden City, NY: Doubleday and Company, Incorporated, 1966

John Paul II, Pope *Blessed Are the Pure of Heart: Catechesis on the Book of Genesis* Vatican trans. Boston, MA: Daughters of St. Paul, 1983

— *Centesimus Annus* Sherbrooke, QC: Editions Paulines, 1991

— 'Discourse to the Members of the 35th General Assembly of the World Medical Association' *AAS*, 76 (1984): 389–395

— *On Human Work: Laborem Exercens* Vatican trans. Boston, MA: St. Paul Editions, 1981

— *On the Christian Meaning of Human Suffering* Vatican trans. Boston, MA: Daughters of St. Paul, 1984

— *Original Unity of Man and Woman: Catechesis on the Book of Genesis* Boston, MA: Daughters of St. Paul, 1981

— 'Population Conference Draft Document Criticized' *Origins*, 23, 41 (March 31, 1994): 716–719

— *Reflections on Humanae Vitae* Vatican trans. Boston, MA: Daughters of St. Paul, 1984

— *The Theology of Marriage and Celibacy* Vatican trans. Boston, MA: Daughters of St. Paul, 1986

— *Veritatis Splendor* Vatican trans. *Origins*, 23, 18 (October 14, 1993): 297–334

Joyce, Robert *Human Sexual Ecology: A Philosophy and Ethics of Man and Woman* Washington, D.C.: University Press of America, 1981

Kardong, Terrence G. 'Chewing the Text: Early Monastic *Lectio Divina* of the Bible.' *The Canadian Catholic Review*, 11, 10 (November, 1993): 7–10

Kasper, Walter *Theology and Church* Margaret Kohl trans. New York: Crossroad Publishing Company, 1989

Knight News Service. '"Aura" Now Thought To Be a Type of Electromagnetic Energy' *The Evening Sun* (April 13, 1978): D1

Lane, Dermot A. 'Anthropology and Eschatology' *Irish Theological Quarterly*, 61, 1 (1995): 14–31

Lederer, Wolfgang *The Fear of Women* New York: Harcourt Brace Jovanovich, Incorporated, 1968

Lejeune, Jerome 'Biological Happening or a Future for Mankind?' and 'Origins of Man' Lectures in McGivney Lecture

Series, co-sponsored by John Paul II Institute and Providence Hospital, Washington, D.C., October 26–29, 1993

Lemonick, Michael D. 'Echoes of the Big Bang' *Time*, 139, 18 (May 4, 1992): 62–63

— 'How Man Began' *Time*, 143, 11 (March 14, 1994): 80–87

Luke, Helen *Old Age* New York: Parabola Books, 1987

Macquarrie, John *Principles of Christian Theology*, 2nd ed. New York: Charles Scribner's Sons, 1977

Maloney, George A. *The Silence of Surrendering Love: Body, Soul, Spirit Integration* New York: Alba House, 1986

Maria Regina Martyrum Raimund Grieger trans. Berlin, 1965

Martin, Francis *The Feminist Question: Feminist Theology in the Light of Christian Tradition* Grand Rapids, MI: William B. Eerdmans Publishing Company, 1994

Martos, Joseph *Doors to the Sacred: A Historical Introduction to the Sacraments in the Catholic Church* Garden City, NY: Doubleday and Company, Incorporated, 1981

May, William *Marriage: The Rock on Which the Family is Built* San Francisco: Ignatius Press, 1995

McCarthy, Timothy 'Reality as Cosmic Dance' *National Catholic Reporter* (December 11, 1987): 7–9, 13

Medieval Women's Visionary Literature Elizabeth Alvilda Petroff ed. Oxford University Press, 1986

Mondin, Battista *The Principle of Analogy in Protestant and Catholic Theology*, 2nd revised ed. The Hague: Martinus Nijhoff, 1968

Morris, Joan *The Lady Was a Bishop: The Hidden History of Women With Clerical Ordination and the Jurisdiction of Bishops* New York: Macmillan Company, 1973

Murchie, Guy *The Seven Mysteries of Life* Boston, MA: Houghton Mifflin Company, 1978

Murray, John Courtney *The Problem of God* New Haven, CT: Yale University Press, 1964

Nuland, Sherwin B. *How We Die: Reflections on Life's Final Chapter* New York: Alfred A. Knopf, 1994

'One Artist's Body of Work' *The Washington Post* (December 26, 1993): C3

O'Neill, Mary Aquin 'The Mystery of Being Human Together,' in *Freeing Theology: The Essentials of Theology in Feminist*

Perspective Catherine Mowry LaCugna ed. San Francisco: HarperCollins Publishers, 1993: 139–160

Palmer, Parker J. 'The Violence of Our Knowledge: Toward a Spirituality of Higher Education' The Michael Keenan Memorial Lecture, St. Thomas More College, University of Saskatchewan, October, 1993

Paul VI, Pope *On the Regulation of Birth: Humanae Vitae* Washington, D.C.: United States Catholic Conference, 1968

Pegis, Anton C. 'St. Thomas and the Unity of Man,' in *Progress in Philosophy* James A. McWilliams ed. Milwaukee: Bruce Publishing Company, 1955: 153–173

Perkins, Pheme 'Gnosticism,' in *The New Dictionary of Theology* Joseph Komanchak, Mary Collins and Dermot E. Lane eds. Wilmington, DE: Michael Glazier, Incorporated, 1987: 421–423

Pius XII, Pope 'Munificentissimus Deus' in *Acta Apostolica Sedis* 42 (November 4, 1950): 753–771

Prokes, Sister Mary Timothy *Mutuality: The Human Image of Trinitarian Love* Mahwah, NJ: Paulist Press, 1993

— *The Flesh Was Made Word* Toronto: Doctoral dissertation, University of St Michael's College, 1976 .

— 'The Nuptial Meaning of Body in Light of Mary's Assumption' *Communio*, 2 (Summer, 1984): 157–176

Rahner, Karl *Mary, Mother of the Lord* New York: Herder and Herder, 1963

— 'On the Theology of the Incarnation' in *Theological Investigations IV* Kevin Smyth trans. London: Darton, Longman and Todd, 1966: 105–120

— 'The Interpretation of the Dogma of the Assumption,' in *Theological Investigations I* Cornelius Ernst trans. Baltimore: Helicon Press, 1961: 215–227

— 'The Theology of the Symbol,' in *Theological Investigations IV* Kevin Smyth trans. London: Darton, Longman and Todd, 1966: 221–252

Rahner, Karl, and Herbert Vorgrimler *Theological Dictionary* Cornelius Ernst ed.; Richard Strachan trans. New York: Herder and Herder, 1965

Ratzinger, Joseph 'Concerning the Notion of Person in Theology' *Communio*, 17 (Fall, 1990): 439–454

Rausch, Thomas P. 'Development of Doctrine,' in *The New Dictionary of Theology* Joseph A. Komonchak, Mary Collins, and Dermot A. Lane eds. Wilmington, DE: Michael Glazier, Incorporated, 1987: 280–283

Robinson, John A. T. *The Body* London: SCM Press, 1952

Roo, William van *Man the Symbolizer* Rome: Gregorian University Press, 1981

Ruffing, Janet 'You Fill Up My Senses: God and Our Senses' *The Way* (April, 1995): 101–110

Ryan, Francis *The Body as Symbol: Merleau-Ponty and Incarnational Theology* Washington, D.C.: Corpus Instrumentorum, Incorporated, 1970

Sawyer, Kathy 'Is It Real or Is It …?' *The Washington Post* (February 21, 1994): A3

Schmaus, Michael *Dogma 2: God and Creation* New York: Sheed and Ward, 1969

Seguin, Michel 'The Biblical Foundations of the Thought of John Paul II on Human Sexuality' *Communio*, xx, 2 (Summer, 1993): 266–289

Shea, George W. 'The Assumption,' in *The Mystery of the Woman* Edward D. O'Connor ed. Notre Dame, IN: Notre Dame University Press, 1956: 65–108

Sheldrake, Rupert *A New Science of Life: The Hypothesis of Formative Causation* Los Angeles: J. P. Tarcher, Incorporated, 1981

Span, Paula 'Dying Is an Art' *The Washington Post* (January 2, 1994): G1, G6

Splett, Jorg 'Body,' in *Sacramentum Mundi I* Karl Rahner, Cornelius Ernst and Kevin Smyth eds. Montreal, QC: Palm Publishers, 1968: 233–235

Stern, Karl *The Flight From Woman* New York: Farrar, Straus and Giroux, 1965

Tertullian *De resurrectione carnis* Ernest Evans ed. London: SPCK, 1960

Thérèse of Lisieux *Story of a Soul: The Autobiography of St. Thérèse of Lisieux*, 2nd ed. John Clarke trans. Washington, D.C.: ICS Publishing, 1976

Vagaggini, Cipriano *The Flesh Instrument of Salvation: A Theology of the Human Body* Charles Underhill Quinn trans. Staten Island, NY: Society of St. Paul, 1969

Vogel, Arthur *Body Theology: God's Presence in Man's World* New York: Harper and Row Publishers, 1973

Wagner, Charles 'Body Totality: The Experience of Phantom Limb Pain. Theological and Pastoral Reflections,' Thesis, Newman Theological College, Edmonton, Alberta, 1992, (microfilm: National Library of Canada)

Wasserman, Aaron O. *Biology* New York: Appleton-Century-Crofts, 1973

Wiles, Maurice 'Christianity Without Incarnation?' in *The Myth of God Incarnate* John Hick ed. Philadelphia, PA: Westminster Press, 1977: 1–10

Woodman, Marion *The Pregnant Virgin: A Process of Psychological Transformation* Toronto: Inner City Books, 1985

Zaner, Richard *The Context of Self: A Phenomenological Inquiry Using Medicine as a Clue* Athens, OH: Ohio University Press, 1981

— *The Problem of Embodiment: Some Contributions to a Phenomenology of the Body*, 2nd ed. The Hague: Martinus Nijhoff, 1971

Index of Names

Index of Subjects